CHRISTIANITY

Volumes in the Religious Traditions of the World Series

Edited by H. Byron Earhart

Religions of Japan *by H. Byron Earhart*
Religions of China *by Daniel L. Overmyer*
Hinduism *by David M. Knipe*
Buddhism *by Robert C. Lester*
Christianity *by Sandra S. Frankiel*
Judaism *by Michael Fishbane*
Islam *by Frederick Denny*
Religions of Africa *by E. Thomas Lawson*
Native Religions of North America *by Åke Hultkrantz*
Religions of Mesoamerica *by David Carrasco*

CHRISTIANITY

A Way of Salvation

SANDRA SIZER FRANKIEL

HarperSanFrancisco
A Division of HarperCollins*Publishers*

Designed by Donna Davis

Library of Congress Cataloging in Publication Data

Frankiel, Sandra Sizer.
    Christianity: a way of salvation.

    (Religious traditions of the world series)

    Bibliography: p.
    Includes index.
    1. Church history. 2. Christian life. I. Title.
BR145.2.F693   1985   270   84–48770
ISBN 0-06-063015-9

91 92 93 94 MUR 12 11 10 9

Contents

Editor's Foreword   ix

Chapter I. Introduction   1

Chapter II. The Historical Development of
Christianity   6

       Organization and Development   11

       The Church in the Later Empire   16

       Eastern and Western Branches of the
       Church   20

       The Western Middle Ages   28

       European Religious Reformation   38

       New Worlds   48

       Modern Developments in Christianity   51

Chapter III. Structures of the Christian Life   57

       The Christian Story   58

       The Meaning of Salvation   59

       Spiritual Knowledge: Creed and Doctrine in
       Christianity   61

       The Drama of Transformation: From Baptism
       to Eucharist   65

       The Church as Holy Community   69

       The Life of the Church   76

Jesus as Model of the Christian's Personal
Life 83

Chapter IV. Dynamics of Christian Life 90

The Pilgrimage to Compostela 91

The Route of the Pilgrim 94

The Meaning of the Pilgrimage 99

Lyman Beecher and Harriet Beecher
Stowe 103

The World of Lyman Beecher 104

Harriet Beecher Stowe 110

American Protestantism in a
New Generation 115

Chapter V. Conclusions 120

Notes 127

Glossary 129

Selected Reading List 134

■

Religious Traditions of the World

O ne of human history's most fascinating aspects is the richness and variety of its religious traditions—from the earliest times to the present, in every area of the world. The ideal way to learn about all these religions would be to visit the homeland of each—to discuss the scriptures or myths with members of these traditions, explore their shrines and sacred places, view their customs and rituals. Few people have the luxury of leisure and money to take such trips, of course; nor are many prepared to make a systematic study of even those religions that are close at hand. Thus this series of books is a substitute for an around-the-world trip to many different religious traditions: it is an armchair pilgrimage through a number of traditions both distant and different from one another, as well as some situated close to one another in time, space, and religious commitment.

Individual volumes in this series focus on one or more religions, emphasizing the distinctiveness of each tradition while considering it within a comparative context. What links the volumes as a series is a shared concern for religious traditions and a common format for discussing them. Generally, each volume will explore the history of a tradition, interpret it as a unified set of religious beliefs and practices, and give examples of religious careers and typical practices. Individual volumes are self-contained treatments and can be taken up in any sequence. They are introductory, providing interested readers with an overall interpretation of religious traditions without presupposing prior knowledge.

The author of each book combines special knowledge of a religious tradition with considerable experience in teaching and communicating an interpretation of that tradition. This special knowledge includes familiarity with various languages, investigation of religious texts and historical development, and direct contact with the peoples and practices under study. The authors have refined their special knowledge through many years of teaching and writing to frame a general interpretation of the tradition that is responsible to the best-known facts and is readily available to the interested reader.

Let me join with the authors of the series in wishing you an enjoyable and profitable experience in learning about religious traditions of the world.

H. Byron Earhart
Series Editor

CHAPTER I

Introduction

B eginning the study of Christianity means opening a door to a world of fascinating figures, paradoxical beliefs, mysterious rites, and unending questions. For Western students especially it is an important enterprise, for Christianity is at once a familiar part of the environment and a hidden influence on our lives. Mention of Christianity often brings powerful questions to the fore: What is the significance, the deep meaning, of Christianity as a religion? How has it been so powerful in people's lives—how did it come to influence millions over two thousand years of history? What importance does it have in my life, in my society and culture? These questions might be asked of any religion, but they have added weight in a society where virtually every day one meets Christian believers and confronts Christian influence in politics, education, and culture. The study of Christianity should provide students with at least some of the resources to answer such questions: basic information about Christianity; a grasp of some of the issues that have been important to Christians; and a sense of the depths of the religion, which have made it a motivating force in people's lives.

First, however, we need to establish a preliminary agreement on what we mean by the term *Christianity*. Most simply, Christianity is the religion of those people who believe in Jesus Christ as the savior of the world. But that immediately raises more questions: Who is Jesus Christ? What is a savior? What is meant by "believe in"?

In fact, we know very little about the man called Jesus Christ—more properly, Jesus the Christ, for "Christ" is derived from the Greek term for **Messiah,*** the anointed one of God. All we know comes from the New Testament writings about him, none earlier

---

*Terms defined in the Glossary are printed in boldface where they first appear in the text.

than about ten years after his death (Paul's letters, and Paul never
knew Jesus alive) and most written down at least thirty years after
his death (the Gospels). He seems to have been a wandering teacher
in Palestine, mostly in Galilee and Samaria, for about three years.
He preached the impending end of the world and the coming **kingdom of God**. He was a powerful teacher and healer, and he probably instituted some customs among his disciples that later became
rituals of the church. He was crucified by the Romans about 29
C.E.[1] More than that we cannot say for certain; we cannot even declare unequivocally which sayings attributed to him are actually his.
Most of what we know as Christian teachings derives from the early
church and the claims it made about Jesus; we cannot know how
much actually came from him.

It is significant, however, that it was a "church," a defined community, that preached and wrote about Jesus. The people who believed in him formed a tightly organized community living a disciplined way of life. Part of Christianity since then has always been the
community. The early Christian creeds, statements of right belief,
referred to the church as the "Holy Church," meaning that their
community was in some important ways separate from the rest of
the world. They believed that they were continuing the mission of
Jesus, preaching the coming kingdom until he returned.

For they believed he was the savior who would return. As a Jewish sect, they adopted one currently popular belief that God would
send a Messiah at the end of time to rule as king over a new, perfect
world. Jesus was that Messiah. But they also held that Jesus' life,
death, and **resurrection** had changed their lives in the present and
ensured their **salvation**. When the end came, some souls would be
condemned to punishment and some saved; those who belonged to
the church would be among the saved. In the present, they already
felt some of the effects of that salvation; they had a foretaste, in the
intense spiritual life that they lived, of what was to come. How Jesus accomplished this was a great mystery, embodied in the rites and
doctrines of the church. It is this mystery of salvation that has stood
at the heart of Christianity for almost all its history.

To "believe in" Jesus meant to accept what the church taught
about him as true, and to act accordingly: to be baptized, to participate in the rites and ongoing life of the church, to live a moral life
according to the church's standards. Belief was the beginning of

Christian life and a central pillar of it, but it led to much more.

Then, what do we mean by the "religion" of those who held these beliefs? We mean the set of practices, beliefs, and institutions that they established to maintain, express, and transmit their tradition. The religion includes the church and its hierarchy, the lay members and the **clergy**, the world view that they held, the rites they performed, the ethics they taught, the doctrinal systems they developed, and the art, literature, and music that they used to express their religious feelings and ideas.

Immediately our scope widens enormously. For Christianity includes all the religious activities undertaken in the name of Christian belief. We soon discover we must speak not of "the church" but of churches, not of Christianity but of "Christianities." From the beginning there were disagreements among Christian churches: Paul disagreed with the church leaders at Jerusalem; the direction of the church at Corinth was different from that of the church at Rome. Dissent and "heresy" (as the church that won called the beliefs of the dissenting group) ran through the early centuries of Christianity—and never stopped. Even while Christians agreed that Jesus was their savior, they disagreed over whether he actually suffered and died on the cross, or only appeared to do so. Even as they agreed that they should celebrate the **Eucharist**, they disagreed over whether **icons**—portraits of Jesus, Mary, angels, and saints— should be used in the worship services. The Christianity of the warrior society of the eighth-century Franks differed sharply from that of the Byzantine Empire at the same period, and both differed from the Christianity of Martin Luther.

A simple view of Christianity dissolves, and the religion of those who believe in Jesus Christ becomes a large family of religious groups. Its history looks more like an evolutionary tree with large and small branches, some stopping abruptly and others remaining small for a while, then suddenly blossoming into many twigs, some of which become substantial branches. The various churches share some features in common some of the time, but one can never be sure that two groups calling themselves Christian will hold the same views of Jesus, of salvation, of belief, or of what is essential to their religion.

Christianity has a deceptively simple core, but is an extremely diverse religion. We can best approach that diversity by a historical study that traces the contours of development, identifies some of the major different religious styles, worldviews, and directions within the religion. This is what we will attempt in Chapter II, beginning not with Jesus but with the earliest Christian communities as they spread from Asia Minor around the Mediterranean. We will see how the churches developed from a small Jewish sect into the official religion of the Roman Empire, and then split again into two great branches, the Eastern and Western, the Orthodox and the Roman Catholic churches. We will trace the history of each branch into the Middle Ages, and after the time of the Crusades, we will follow the development of the Western church through the Reformation, the translation of Christianity to many peoples of the world, and the emergence of modern Christianity. In each case we will be attempting to capture the religious spirit of the age, the style and worldview as much as the events and people that are the highlights of the period.

Because it accentuates diversity, however, history is only one dimension of any study of religion. There are also features that endure over time, which seem characteristic of one particular religion over against others. These we treat in Chapter III. These basic structures of Christianity also have their historical dimension, of course; practices change, people develop new interpretations of old features; some aspects decline in importance as others rise to prominence. Yet most of the elements that we would call basic structures appear in the early development of the religion and remain, even if only in fragmentary form, throughout most of the life of the religion.

Many of these enduring structures, moreover, are those that have counterparts in other religions. To mention just a few examples: rituals of immersion in water and of sacred communal meals are common to many traditions; the idea of a holy community or holy people appears in some; the tension between the present world and an ideal state beyond, expressed in the Christian idea of salvation, is familiar to believers in different religions. It would be a mistake, however, to begin comparing these in isolation. The point is not that Christianity is like or unlike Buddhist, Judaic, or Ashanti tradition on any given point. Rather, the enduring structures of Christianity point to a ground that various religions share, where one can locate the deeper impulses of any religion. In other words, these enduring structures suggest the depth of Christianity's power as a religion, operating below the surface changes of history. Christianity, of course, expresses and shapes these common impulses in its own distinctive way: salvation is not the same as enlightenment in Buddhism; the Eucharist is not equivalent to ancient practices of sacrifice. The deeply embedded common structures interact with the historical particularities to produce a distinctive religion. So we must learn to stretch our minds here to encompass both the universal and the particular religious impulses expressed in Christian religious structures.

We will take yet a third approach to understanding in Chapter IV, filling out our outline of history and structure by looking at two specific examples of Christian belief and practice in a time of significant change. One example will be a twelfth-century pilgrimage to the Roman Catholic shrine of Saint James of Compostela in Spain. The second takes place within a family famous in nineteenth-century American religion, in which a daughter, Harriet Beecher Stowe, struggles with her spiritual inheritance with her father, Lyman Beecher. Both examples will give us brief but valuable glimpses into the rich and intricate dynamics of Christian life, showing us the interweaving of traditional beliefs and practices with new thoughts, desires, and goals. The final chapter will offer some general observations about Christianity and set forth a few of the problems faced by modern Christians.

This multidimensional approach aims to provide a rich picture of Christianity by utilizing a variety of perspectives, bringing some material into view more than once to reinforce learning and provoke questions. The student should be forewarned, however, that no book on so large a subject can be exhaustive. It is to be hoped that readers will supplement this book with some readings in primary text material, to encounter at first hand the words of Christians speaking for themselves about their beliefs, arguing with one another, praying, or singing. Such readings will enliven the discussion in the text and provide points of entry for deeper study and for questioning the interpretations put forward here.

For this book is also meant to be argued with. History is being rewritten every day; our understanding of religion itself is undergoing dramatic change in this generation. As something to argue with, this book will serve a much greater purpose than it can by simply being read from an interested distance.

CHAPTER II

The Historical Development of Christianity

The religion we know as Christianity originated as a small sect within the religion of Judaism, in the fourth decade of the first century. In the years 30–100 C.E. small groups of interested Jews and Gentiles were beginning to gather themselves as a distinct body within Judaism, both in Palestine and in the larger Roman Empire. At the outset these groups kept many of the Jewish practices of their times: they observed some of the dietary laws and the Sabbath (Saturday), celebrated the major festivals, and honored the Holy Temple in Jerusalem, although they probably paid little attention to the priestly rituals of purity. Yet they had certain peculiarities: the members gathered also on Sunday, the first day of the week, for a common meal culminating in a ritual of bread and wine, and all members would have undergone a special ritual immersion, or **baptism**, before being admitted to their first ritual meal.

These new additions to Jewish ritual life were connected to a remarkable set of beliefs. The ritual immersion was a baptism of repentance: those who had repented of all their **sins** and turned to a new life would be cleansed in the natural waters of a river or lake. Just as many Jews, then and now, practiced immersion before Yom Kippur (the Day of Atonement, when they believe all people are judged for their sins), so these sectarian Jews immersed themselves in preparation for the final Day of Judgment, the great Yom Kippur that would mark the end of the present world.

For their **eschatology** held that the world as we know it was about to end. A new world would soon be ushered in with the return of God's Messiah (Greek *Christos*, source of our word

"Christ"), that is, God's chosen king. These new believers came to be called Christians, that is, believers in the Messiah. They claimed that the Christ had in fact appeared on earth already in the form of a man named Jesus, who had been killed by the Romans, crucified as a suspected political rebel. His followers believed he had been resurrected after three days—a development of the belief held by many Jews that the messianic age would include a general resurrection of the dead. Jesus had then returned to be with God in heaven. His suffering or "Passion," death, and resurrection signified a complete victory over sin and evil in the world, ensuring the salvation of all believers; soon he would return to earth, judge the world, and inaugurate God's kingdom. The Christians' ritual of bread and wine harked back to a practice Jesus was said to have instituted among his first followers, to eat the bread as his body and the wine as his blood, reminding themselves of him and his death until he returned. Sunday was the "Lord's day," the day on which the resurrection from the tomb was said to have taken place.

Such a sect was not necessarily a startling new development. Like other religions of the time, Judaism had become preoccupied with the question of salvation: how were people to redeem themselves from this evil world? Different groups offered different answers. A number of sects awaited the coming of a Messiah who would restore independence to the land of Israel, either by force or by a spiritual hand. The Zealots, for example, looked toward political revolution as a means of ushering in the messianic era. Later, around 130–35 C.E., many Jews, including important rabbis, pinned their hopes on a man named Bar Kochba as the Messiah who would lead the final revolt against Rome. From at least the first century B.C.E. a quiet, ascetic Jewish community called the Essenes, living near the Dead Sea, anticipated a final war between the Sons of Light and the Sons of Darkness, with leadership by one or more messianic figures. A prophetic man known as John the Baptist preached repentance and the coming kingdom of God during Jesus' lifetime; indeed, Christian tradition holds that Jesus was baptized by John, in effect continuing John's mission. Some baptist groups, perhaps including John's, believed in a supernatural being who occasionally came to earth as a divine incarnation to reveal God's will. Besides this, groups of Jews and non-Jews often gathered for table-fellowship, sharing a common meal in a ritual way. The new Jewish group who believed in a crucified Messiah was therefore unique in some ways, but not so much as to stand out in a society of such diverse religious preferences as first-century Judaism.

What soon began to make the Christians more noticeable was their intense **evangelizing** activity. Judaism had long made it a practice to accept converts, and in the Hellenistic period some Jews actively sought out Gentiles who would come to learn Jewish wisdom in the synagogues. Synagogue membership usually included a number of converts plus a number of "God-fearers," as they were called, who supported the synagogue and learned there without completing the conversion process (which included **circumcision** and ritual immersion). Jews and non-Jews, therefore, frequently intermingled.

Christians, however, took on an active missionary effort far beyond what Jews had ever done. The original followers of Jesus, including the **apostles** and other early adherents, became wandering teachers and healers. Convinced that the world was about to end, with a strong inner sense of living in virtually another world already, they traveled about, preaching the "gospel" or "good news" that the Messiah of God had appeared on earth and all should repent of their sins. Like Jesus, they claimed to be able to heal and to exorcise demons (which were believed to cause some illnesses), and by healing people they demonstrated their power over the present evil world. Throughout the Roman Empire, from Asia Minor to Spain, they taught in or near synagogues and organized new communities of believers.

Why the Christians became such thoroughgoing evangelists has been an interesting question for historians. The Gospel of Matthew, one of the documents of the New Testament, records that Jesus said, "Go therefore and make disciples of all nations," but that saying may well be the later addition of an already evangelistic church, imputed to Jesus. What is clear is that the early followers possessed a strong sense of a divine spirit and that some had healing powers, both of which would be conducive to spreading the faith. But the missionary impulse outlasted the first few generations. The historian John Gager has argued, on the basis of comparison with sociological studies of messianic or **millenarian** groups, that the disappointment of Christian expectations that the world would soon end was a primary factor in the impulse to proselytize. If believers had questions about the return of the Messiah, they might subdue their inner doubts by increasing the strength of their group. The group could continue, vital and growing, even though the Messiah did not return. In any case, the missionary outlook did prevail. The failure of Christ to return did not provoke a great crisis in the church, and the evangelical attitude became deeply ingrained in the Christian tradition.

Christian missions gradually succeeded in establishing the new religion throughout the empire, increasingly among non-Jews rather than Jews. The written documents of early Christians, especially the letters of Paul and the Book of Acts (by the same author as the Gospel of Luke), reveal many issues raised in the first generation about the admission of non-Jews, particularly how much of Jewish law they should observe. In the time of Paul's ministry, after heated arguments, the churches dropped the requirement of circumcision and modified the dietary laws, making it easier for Gentiles to enter. Both Gentile and Jewish Christians undertook a lengthy period of study, usually almost a year, before baptism. They studied the Bible—that is, the Jewish Bible in Greek translation, known as the Septuagint. Presumably they learned the outline of the legends and records of Jewish history and the Christian interpretation of the Hebrew prophets. (Christians read the prophetic words about God's chosen king as referring to Jesus. Jews understood the same texts differently; in some cases they did not understand them to be messianic in meaning at all.) New Christians may also have learned secret or mystical interpretations of Jesus and of Christian rites.

The predominantly non-Jewish environment and membership of most churches, combined with their use of a Greek translation, meant that Hellenistic interpretations deeply influenced the basic beliefs of the church. Even the basic assertion that Jesus was God's chosen would be understood differently by non-Jews than by Jews. For example, many other Hellenistic religions believed in a savior figure, divine or semi-divine, who would save human beings from the evils of this world and transport them to a heavenly realm beyond the planetary spheres. As Christianity quickly spread away from Palestine (which itself was influenced by Greek culture), the Jewish messianic idea of a human king divinely chosen to rule on earth combined with, or gave way to, the Hellenistic view that "Jesus the Christ" was a divine savior from the heavens. On this view,

belief in Christ as divine, together with repentance from sin and acceptance of the rites of the church, could bring assurance of "salvation"—eternal life in an otherworldly sense—when Jesus returned.

Early believers also developed new interpretations of the **Holy
Spirit**. Tradition held that when Jesus' followers gathered in Jerusalem for the Jewish festival of Shavuot ("Weeks," being seven weeks
after the beginning of Passover, and called Pentecost by Greek-
speaking Jews), they received the Holy Spirit. Tongues of fire
seemed to appear over their heads, and they began prophesying or
"speaking in **tongues**"—probably an outpouring of language-like
sounds or words in known or unknown languages. This outburst of
ecstatic speech, not at all unusual in new, enthusiastic spiritual communities, marked in Christian tradition the occasion of God's send-
ing his Spirit on the church to guide it until Jesus returned. The
Holy Spirit became God's manifestation on earth, eventually regarded as part of the **Trinity** of Father, Son, and Holy Spirit, which
were the three manifestations of God's self-revelation. The church
itself as recipient of the Holy Spirit, and especially its leaders to
whom authority had been given by laying on of hands, represented
God's activity on earth.

Thus the early Christian churches constituted enthusiastic, often
"spirit-filled" communities. Living in high expectation of a glorious
world to come, blessed with gifts of healing and spiritual ecstasy,
they often felt they lived in a new world already by their faith in the
Christ. Originally a Jewish sect, they quickly made their own new
practices central and gradually dropped many of the observances
that made them distinctively Jewish. Of course, many elements inherited from Judaism remained in the **liturgy** and in theological
attitudes. Keeping the Jewish Bible as a basic text ensured some
continuity. Increasingly, however, Christianity followed its own way,
cutting its ties to traditions of Jewish learning and, indeed, often
turning against its parent tradition. Christianity's relative lack of
success among Jews led some early writers to castigate the Jews for
rejecting Jesus, wrongly accusing them of responsibility for Jesus'
death. Also, Christians had to defend their faith against Roman
misunderstanding: how could they claim to be carriers of the true
Jewish faith (as they did in order to claim freedom of worship) while
supplanting the practices of the ancestral religion? Together with the
psychological difficulties of individuals who were departing from

their mother religion, these factors planted in the writings that became part of the Christian Bible the seeds of antagonism that would
later support Christian anti-Semitism. The great spiritual ecstasy
and evangelical passion that characterized early Christianity thus had
also a dark side in antagonism toward Jews.

Organization and Development

The first century of Christianity, until about 150 C.E., saw the
expansion of the earliest small, dedicated groups into larger groups
of converted Jews and Gentiles—and eventually groups not identified as Jewish at all—dotted throughout the cities and larger towns
of the empire. In Palestine, where Christianity was important before
70 C.E., members were mostly villagers; outside that land converts
were mostly from the urban middle class. At first, wandering
preachers led the congregations, but soon settled local leadership
emerged. Early groups gathered in homes on Sunday mornings.
Roles were assigned to keep order because of the great spiritual excitement in some churches and the debates and disputations in others. "Teachers" emerged as the primary local leaders, and evangelists
continued traveling on missions. The **deacon** was one of the local
leaders responsible for managing the ritual and perhaps for other
administrative duties. This became the lowest priestly office (that is,
an office requiring the laying on of hands by a bishop). Women
were prominent as teachers in the early church but were not allowed
to rise higher than the level of deacon; in later generations men appropriated even that role to themselves alone. The central figure in
any community was the **bishop**, originally elected by all the Christians in a given city (as determined by the Roman city boundaries).
The bishop, as spiritual head of the church, celebrated the ritual of
bread and wine for the entire community until it became too large
to gather in one building. He selected and ordained, by laying on of
hands, priests to be his assistants, and as the community grew,
priests celebrated the Eucharist for outlying churches. Gradually, a
greater hierarchy emerged, in some respects parallel to that of the
empire. The bishop of the capital city of a Roman province became
the center of power for his province. By the third century there were
four centers of power in the church: Jerusalem, Antioch (in Syria),

Alexandria (in Egypt), and Rome. The bishop of each, called a **patriarch**, held authority coordinate with the three others. After the reign of Constantine and the establishment of Constantinople (formerly Byzantium) as the new capital in his name, that city and Rome began to move into prominence ahead of the others. By this time, the fourth century, Christianity had a strongly organized government of municipalities with a great deal of power vested in the upper levels.

During the first three centuries the literature that eventually became the New Testament was written, copied, and shared among the churches. (All the early churches also used the Jewish Bible—Torah, Prophets, and Writings—which came to be known as the Old Testament.) The earliest Christian literature known to us is the letters of Paul, written during his missionary work between 40 and 60 C.E. Shortly afterward came the Gospels, which are stories of Jesus' life, and Acts, telling of the deeds of the early apostles.[2] The various other letters come from the late first or early second century, some of them written in the name of Paul to enhance their authority. The Book of Revelation, in the form of an **apocalypse**, probably was written down shortly after 100 C.E. Christian communities also produced other works not in the New Testament—other gospels, letters, acts, and apocalypses. But because of their small circulation, lack of apostolic authority, or late composition, the organized Christian church did not include them when, in the third and fourth centuries, it began to draw together its body of holy literature.

Also in the first three centuries Christian liturgy began to take shape. Originally Christians gathered on Sunday mornings for a common meal that included the rite of bread and wine, that is, the Eucharist or "thanksgiving." Soon this rite was separated from the rest of the meal, the *agape* or communal love-feast, which was more casual. The Eucharist took center stage; it became the primary Christian **sacrament**, a rite of great spiritual power that communicated **grace** by re-enacting the savings acts of Jesus himself. For most of Christian history this ritual has been regarded as a mysterious and indeed **mystical** sharing in the body and blood of Christ. In Chapter III, we will see in greater detail its significance; for now, it is sufficient to note that the Eucharist became the central act around which an entire liturgy evolved: prayers, hymns of glory and thanksgiving, Scripture readings, and sermons.

In many respects, then, the churches were moving toward uniformity in rite and literature and toward hierarchy in organization. Yet Christianity included a great deal of diversity well into the third century. The variety of literature circulated in the early years is one indication of differences among communities; also, Paul's letters show that each church had its own spiritual, theological, and organizational problems. From the second century onward, Christians tended to express such differences in debates over doctrine. In the philosophically oriented Hellenistic world, it was expected that any sophisticated religion would develop a body of correct, rational thought. However, in Christianity it was not always easy to agree on a single formulation of religious wisdom; so various Christian theologies emerged, some of which actually split the churches into hostile factions.

In the second century some groups of Christians claimed a special knowledge, or *gnosis*, apart from the written literature and traditions handed down to the bishops (presumably from Jesus' first apostles). Most of these Gnostics, as they were called, believed that the world was created by, and under the control of, an evil god. The true God was totally separate from any material creation and was known only through special spiritual revelation. Marcion, a Christian leader from Asia Minor who preached in Rome in the second century, argued, for example, that the church should not keep the Old Testament because it was the book of the evil creator God. In the middle of the third century, another leader arose in the East, the prophet Mani (d. 276), who called himself Apostle of Jesus Christ. Mani taught that the universe was divided into the forces of Light and Darkness and that the God of Light had sent many messengers to human beings, but the most perfect of these was Jesus, a truly divine being who only seemed to be mortal and material. Thanks to Jesus, the fragments of Light in the souls of humans could be caught up after death, distilled, and returned to the realms of Light.

Both Marcion and Mani gained many followers (even Augustine, later the great orthodox bishop and theologian, spent nearly ten years as a Manichee). Manichean churches were powerful down to the sixth century, and in the eastern regions even to the year 1000. The orthodox churches eventually succeeded in establishing their primacy, however. By the fourth century most Christians had come to agree that Jesus was both human and divine, the "son" of the good God who had created the world. Yet there were still arguments: How exactly was Jesus related to God? If he was divine, were there two Gods? Or was he less than God, as some statements in Scripture seemed to indicate (e.g., "My Father is greater than I").

Such questions led to another series of controversies, the most important one beginning in fourth-century Alexandria. There a church elder named Arius argued that Christ was different from God, indeed was created at a certain point in time by God. Christ was not a mere man—rather, he was the Logos, the first principle of the cosmos, a primary angelic being through whom all else was created—but he was clearly a creature. The bishop's secretary (later bishop himself), Athanasius, claimed that Arius's view threatened the idea of salvation through Christ. For if Christ were merely a creature, he might even turn evil (as angelic beings had been known to do). Therefore Christ was not created but begotten, generated, from God himself. Soon, bishops and elders in many churches lined up on either side of the argument.

Constantine, who did not well understand why his subjects were quibbling over such a point, called a council in 325, the Council of Nicea, to settle the dispute. The bishops decided in favor of Athanasius, but the Arians continued to win adherents—including later emperors. Over the next few decades, Athanasius would be exiled four times for his views. And at one point when Arians were in control, missionaries were sent west who converted some of the warrior societies to an Arian version of Christianity—a fact that caused difficulties centuries later in their coming to terms with Rome. The controversy shows how fervently Christians argued about doctrine—and how each argument could send ripples through the entire empire.

Yet, despite such controversies, the Christian churches within the empire did remain conscious of their underlying unity. One important factor in creating this consciousness was pressure from outside. Competition with numerous religious groups—Judaism, Hellenistic mystery cults, the worship of traditional Roman gods—pressured each group to define itself clearly. Christians defined themselves in relation to Judaism by recognizing their parent tradition, and tried to claim they should enjoy the protected status of an "ancestral religion" so that under Roman law they would be allowed freedom of worship. They never gained that status, however, because Rome saw them as rejecting much of Jewish practice.

In relation to other religions, Christians took the high road by entering into dialogue and debate with the Greek philosophical tradition that dominated the educational system of the empire. In the second century Justin Martyr developed an "**Apology**" for Christianity as *the* true philosophy in the Greek sense. He claimed that Christ was the manifest Logos, known to the Greeks as the first principle of the cosmos, that is, Wisdom. Socrates, he said, had known the Logos, so in effect he had known Christ. This "Logos theology" was highly influential in defining Christian doctrine—as we saw, Arius used the idea in his theology. Later, the great scholar Origen of Alexandria (ca. 185—c. 254) argued that Christianity was the culmination of all civilized culture; and Eusebius of Caesarea (263–339), the first church historian, propagandized for Christianity among the educated public—including his friend the emperor Constantine. The apologists thus paved the way for Christianity to become acceptable and powerful in the empire by enlarging the philosophical scope of the religion. And though these thinkers were often engaged in internal disputes, they also helped weld the churches together by uniting Christian ideas with the best of current Greek thought.

Persecution was another factor in promoting Christian unity, although its significance has sometimes been exaggerated. Christians came under attack as early as Nero's reign (54–68 C.E.), but that persecution and most others in the first two centuries were local and short-lived. By the middle of the third century, however, Christianity had become strong enough to come into direct conflict with Roman imperial religion, and that was when serious and thorough persecution, as a matter of imperial policy, began. At that time, in the face of increasingly serious threats, the empire had to inculcate at least a minimal patriotism to forge some unity among the diverse cultures of the Mediterranean. The worship of traditional Roman gods and of the emperor served this function, while bringing some added economic benefits through donations and sacrifices. New laws therefore required Christians to sacrifice to the emperor; if they refused, they were subject to imprisonment or death. Some did sacrifice; some bought illegally a certificate stating they had performed the ritual. Others, upholding the church's view that such a practice compromised their allegiance to God, were persecuted under Decius (249–51), Diocletian (284–305), and Galerius (305–11 in the eastern half of the empire).

The persecutions, especially Diocletian's, shook the churches badly. Yet at the same time they publicized Christian beliefs and added to the church's list of heroes, exemplars of true faith: the martyrs (from the Greek *martyros*, "witnesses"). The martyrs followed in the footsteps of Jesus and of the first apostles; their suffering, like his, renewed the spiritual power of the church. The authority of their teachings and writings increased; and they were believed to ascend directly to heaven at death—unlike the ordinary believer, who had to wait for the return of Christ. Together with the early apostles and church fathers, they became the great saints of Christianity. As we will see, their power after death, enshrined in their **relics**, helped sustain believers in their faith.

The Church in the Later Empire

By the late third century Christians still numbered a minority of the population of the Roman Empire. Nevertheless, they were respectable and their churches soundly established, having proven their staying power in the competitive world of late Roman religion. Especially in Syria and Asia Minor, the Christian cult had grown dramatically in the previous hundred years. When in the late second century barbarian invasions and plagues threatened many cities, Christians had provided for their own poor, for widows, orphans, and the sick; they offered social and economic security in a world that had become less stable. This intense communal orientation, partly an inheritance from Judaism, distinguished Christianity from other Hellenistic religions and made it more successful than, say, Manicheanism. Other cults also offered such benefits as life after death or protection from demons, but they gave far less support to their members during their earthly lives. In Christianity many people found a firm social grounding, a stimulating intellectual life, a rich and dramatic liturgy, able leaders dedicated to the spiritual life, heroes to admire and emulate, and a hope for a future life beyond the grave.

Shortly, events put the capstone on the growing power of the Christians. Hardly had the persecution of Galerius ended when, in 312, the new emperor, Constantine, took a highly favorable attitude toward the Christians. Having received help in winning a battle from a deity he referred to as the "Unconquerable Sun" (possibly Mithra), he soon found himself persuaded by Christian apologists that indeed this deity had to be the one God in Christ. He agreed to patronize the Christian church, although he also continued to support pagan temples. With this move he gained considerable support among the urban population, countering the strength of his Eastern rival, Licinius. The outcome was that Christianity came to occupy a far more powerful position in the empire. No great influx of converts occurred, but wealth and influence shifted so that, over the next several generations, Christian bishops gained the eminence that Roman senators had once had. Christian celebrations gradually edged out traditional Roman ones, and the power of the churches superseded that of the influential pagan families of the empire.

Nevertheless, at the same time a number of critics had begun to question the worldly success of the churches and their growing interest in honors and prestige. Those who sought a higher spiritual life, a greater closeness to God, began to look elsewhere. Elsewhere, it turned out, was away from the cities entirely, in the desert. In 269 an eighteen-year-old Egyptian named Anthony declared his intention of battling with the demons alone, first on the fringes of his village, then farther into the desert. From 285 until his death in 356 (at the age of 105) he lived weeks from the nearest town, braving the elements and the demonic forces that appeared to him in the most terrifying forms. Athanasius, patriarch of Alexandria, wrote a biography of Anthony that spread the legend of his trials and victories. Before long, Christians in Mesopotamia, Syria, Armenia, and Egypt were leaving the centers of Mediterranean culture to become hermits of various styles.

In Syria the new seekers tended to become wandering holy men, wild and startling in appearance and behavior but revered by the villagers. Some adopted special disciplines, like Simeon Sytlites (296–459), who sat atop a tall pillar for thirty years. At times as many as two thousand people gathered at the base to be near such holiness. The emperor finally had to ask him to come down, for the crowds were a public nuisance. But it was to him and others like

him that the people brought their prayers, their arguments to be
settled, and their children to be blessed. In Egypt, by contrast, the
new **monasticism** took a communal turn. A farmer named Pachomius (ca. 290–347) created a community in the desert by linking
monks' cells and providing a system of mutual support for the hermits. By the year 400 there were seven thousand monks living in
Pachomius's establishment. Again, they were the object of veneration from the townsfolk, who admired their courage and religious
dedication.

The monastic movement and the emergence of holy men affected
all of Christianity. Western bishops often distrusted the new movement, but a few leading churchmen—Ambrose in Milan (Italy),
Martin of Tours (Gaul), and Augustine of Hippo (North Africa)—
supported monastic developments in the late fourth century. In the
East, the holy men were respected and feared by people of all social
ranks. In effect, monks and hermits became the new models of mar-
tyrdom as the church conquered the imperial world. The battle
against paganism, exemplified in the martyrs, was over. Now a different battle began with less tangible forces of evil, namely, the demonic forces that infected people and threatened their souls.
Wealth, sexuality, any kind of worldly appetite could become a
great temptation. Monks exemplified their conquest of the world
and their otherworldly power by being celibate, eating little and
fasting frequently, and living an impoverished life without care for
worldly comforts. Constantly before them stood the great goal: to
persevere in the battle, to win the race, to overcome through great
personal ordeals. Their persistence in the life of perfection, Christians believed, brought them closer to Christ and to God and assured them final victory on the Day of Judgment.

Monks brought spiritual power through their battles in the desert, and bishops and new Christian aristocrats brought it to the upper echelons of the empire, but another sort of holy personage extended the benefits of Christian power to all: the dead holy one, that
is, the saint. Those who had died as martyrs or performed great
miracles became available to Christians on earth as heavenly friends,
as protectors or patrons. Their graves were holy sites and their relics—bones, teeth, or pieces of clothing—were holy remnants that
still carried the personal power of the saint. The veneration of relics
grew so popular that bishops even ordered tombs opened so that

saints' remains could be transported to various parts of the empire; wealthy Christians would then build new shrines for the relics. Pagan families had often held ritual meals at the graves of their ancestors; now bishops began to celebrate the Mass at the graves of saints—the honored spiritual "ancestors" of the Christian "family." Later, churches put relics under their altars as a kind of foundation stone for the holiness of the church itself, or encased them in jeweled boxes to be displayed behind the altar. Relics attracted devotion from people at all levels of society for hundreds of years.

Christian political power, the ascetic movement, and devotion to relics all signaled a gradual unification of fourth- and fifth-century Christianity. Roman paganism lost ground, and sectarian Christian groups found it increasingly difficult to make headway against orthodoxy, as the "catholic" church became in fact the "universal" church of the empire. One of the landmarks of this development was the life and work of Augustine, bishop of Hippo in North Africa. First a Platonist and then a Manichee, Augustine converted to Catholicism and became a political and intellectual leader of the first rank. In the early years of the fifth century he was influential in helping the orthodox defeat a competing African church, that of the Donatists, that claimed it was the true, pure church because its bishops had never given in to persecutors. Later he was involved in an important theological controversy over the extent to which human beings have free will in achieving salvation. Augustine held a doctrine of **predestination**, that God had determined the fate of each soul from the beginning; his chief opponent, Pelagius, argued that individuals are free to accept or reject God's grace.

From about 413 onward Augustine began writing his great work *De Civitate Dei (On the City of God)*, answering pagan charges that Christianity had weakened the empire. Augustine argued that all worldly states and empires, including Rome, are corruptible and ultimately will die; only the City of God is eternal. Christians therefore reside as aliens in this world; their true home is that eternal city that awaits them after this life. Pagans invest too much in this world, which, beautiful though it is, is transient and full of suffering, marred by the divine punishment of Adam's sin. Christians who long for the other world have as their protector and guard the church and its sacraments, for the church is a shadow here on earth of the true heavenly city. This attitude toward the church and the world was satisfying to Augustine's generation, troubled by the incursions of barbarians and the economic ups and downs of late imperial society. It also offered a basis for a continued critique of the world, and as such his work has been a resource for theologians down through the centuries. The *City of God* marked the unification of Christianity as a religion in this world, promoting good order on earth, but with aspirations that went far beyond the ordinary round of life.

Yet, at the same time, Christians were beginning to regard the state itself and the emperor as sacred; and the unity that Augustine expressed was melting away in the heat of the growing differences between East and West. Augustine himself could barely read Greek, the language of the eastern half of the empire and of many great thinkers of the time; and most Greek thinkers would never become interested in his doctrine of predestination.

Eastern and Western Branches of the Church

The links among Christian institutions—monasteries, shrines, churches—formed an interlocking network that crisscrossed the entire Roman Empire. Yet a rift was forming that would eventually undermine the broad cultural continuity of Mediterranean Christianity. Before 400 C.E. the most important boundaries seemed those between south and north, between the "civilized" Mediterranean world and the "barbarian" kingdoms of Europe. That border gradually eroded in favor of one between the East, centered in Constantinople (formerly Byzantium, where Constantine had moved his capital), and the West, centered in Rome, where the western patriarch kept his seat.

The West had been more recently Christianized, for the Roman senators and upper classes had remained loyal to the worship of the Roman gods. Moreover, the West was threatened earlier by barbarians who wanted to enter the wealthy Mediterranean world. Christian leaders in the West therefore felt more precarious in their positions, and they built a strong organization of the elite that, much like the old Senate, sharply defined its own status. Wandering holy men and monks were not so welcome in the West, unless they submitted to the power of Rome. As for the martyred saints, they were, as the historian Peter Brown has put it, safely dead, and the hierarchy could control their shrines. In general, holiness was more clearly the monopoly of the church hierarchy—priests, bishops, and the patriarch of Rome, who came to be called the pope (i.e., "father.").

In the East, by contrast, there was still a strong emperor (Rome's last had been a boy, Romulus Augustus, in 476), and the Eastern emperor occupied a semi-priestly position. He could not perform sacraments or alter the **dogma** formulated by councils, but he could preach, hold the Eucharistic cup of wine in his own hands, and cense the altar during the **Mass**. Other laymen as well were more powerful in the East, for they could participate in church councils. Thus lay power permeated the church, and religious power permeated all of society, for a variety of monks and holy men inhabited villages and towns throughout the countryside. Christian spirituality was more generally accessible, not primarily the possession of the elite: there could be direct human contact with the holy. Indeed, one of the teachings of the Eastern church was that "God became Man, that men might become God."

These differences made for different religious emphases and styles of spirituality. The West focused on the grandeur and awe of the work of God in the world, particularly in the sacrifice of himself, in Christ, for the sake of all humanity. A strong awareness of sin marked the distance between an ordinary human life and a life of true holiness. Yet, because of the great miracle of Christ's sacrifice, human beings could be freed from sin. The Eucharist repeated this most awesome act; it was to be performed with utmost correctness. The emphasis on sacrifice, on purification from sin, and on perfection in ritual created an atmosphere of deep dignity and reverence that has been the hallmark of the Western liturgy. Moreover, in the rest of human life perfection was the goal, to be achieved through discipline, order, and obedience in an attitude of humility. The West thus came to focus on church order, exemplified in the development of church law and legal interpretation of Christian doctrines. (The tradition of Rome itself contributed to this, of course, for the Roman legal system was unsurpassed in the ancient world.) Ultimately, the emphasis on personal discipline, purification, and correct action in ritual and the rest of life served the church well in its encounters with the non-Christian kingdoms to the north and west.

Such themes were by no means absent in the East, but the

Orthodox church focused more on the mystical goal of Christian life: the knowledge of God, unity with Christ, unity with the divine. The accent was on deification more than purification. The whole people participated in the process of deification through the Divine Liturgy and the veneration of icons. The Eucharist in the Orthodox church was more than a sacrifice to cleanse from sin; partaking of Christ's body and blood enabled one to share his humanity united with his divinity. In addition, the celebration was conceived as a wedding feast, in which the church below joined with the holy assembly of saints above in a foretaste of the future transformation of the world when Christ returned.

The heavenly host themselves were present, represented in the icons: portraits of angels, Christ, the Virgin, and saints that stood in the front of the church, between the people and the altar. The originals of many of these paintings were believed to be miraculous appearances; the paintings themselves had to be prepared according to precise ritual, as exact copies of the originals. The icon could be venerated by bowing and kissing because it was believed to be a faithful representation of a heavenly archetype, so true to the divine that it was an earthly reflection of God himself. Indeed, the entire theology of Orthodoxy could be said to be iconic in tone. Each person was believed to have an image or icon of God within him- or herself; the Bible, like an icon, was a faithful reflection of the heavenly "book" of God now made present in words accessible to the worshiper. God becoming human had meant the revelation of the divine energies throughout the world, concentrated with special intensity in the church, its liturgy, and its icons. The Eastern church thus nourished a sense of the continuing transformation of human beings through the divine presence, whereas the West encouraged human striving for perfection through discipline, humility, and sacrifice.

The differences between East and West sharpened as the centuries passed. On the one hand, their different structures of power led to competition between the Roman pope and the Eastern emperor. The pope believed that only he, as the highest churchman, should direct the goals and aims of Christian society; any king was to be the church's protector and the executor of the pope's policies. The emperor saw himself as part priest, part king, and in all ways suited to rule all of society, settling its policies and making its laws. The church should perform its special task of maintaining a proper relationship with God, but it should not rule. On the other hand, each branch of the church had to deal with very different problems. In the West the barbarian invasions took precedence: in the fifth and sixth centuries various societies on the perimeters of the empire attacked Rome, southern Italy, Africa, and Gaul (roughly equivalent to modern France). From then on, the popes and their missionaries had to deal with European societies that were, from their viewpoint, primitive and pagan, and in any case very different from urban, literate Christianity. The Eastern church faced Persia, a sophisticated society, with its mixture of Zoroastrian and mystical traditions, and then later confronted Islam. Both were literate, imperialistic societies with their own high theologies and ethics. As a result, differences between East and West grew; the two branches of Christianity maintained contact, but their interaction had little lasting significance until the time of the Crusades.

The Eastern church was part of an empire, the Byzantine, that

This Byzantine icon from the late thirteenth century shows the Madonna and Child on a curved throne. Used by permission of the National Gallery of Art, Washington, D.C.; Andrew W. Mellon Collection.

went on continuously for many centuries after the decline of the Western capital, indeed, its government and economy functioned more effectively for a longer period of time (over seven centuries) than any other state in history. Thus, whereas some historians have seen a sharp break in Christian history after the fall of Rome, it is preferable to see the Eastern church as the continuation of imperial Christianity. Doctrinal controversy continued: the fifth through the seventh centuries saw the church preoccupied with the Arian issue, and then with a new heresy known as the Monophysite (from the Greek, meaning "one nature"). The Monophysites objected to the accepted formulation of the church (since the Council of Chalcedon in the fourth century) that Christ was of two natures: "truly human, truly divine." They held that he could only be divine, and his divine nature had absorbed the humanity in him. Later, in the eighth and ninth centuries, the church faced a great storm over the use of icons. Influenced by Muslim sentiments against images, the emperor Leo III ordered in 726 that all holy images of Christ, the **Virgin**, and the saints be destroyed. Opposition came from the monks, the people, and the western pope. Icons were restored by the empress Irene in 787, but later emperors renewed Leo's order; only in 843 did the empress Theodora restore them again, finally ending the controversy.

These issues suggest the continuing tension in the church over the nature of divinity and the nature of holiness. The rise of the new and powerful religion of Islam in the seventh century accentuated such issues. For the prophet Muhammad and his successors adopted a strongly Semitic view of these matters, not unlike that of the ancient Hebrew prophets: There was only one God; only he was divine. Human beings could not achieve divinity. Images of God were absolutely forbidden. Many Christians in Asia Minor had also held similar views, and they tried to reform their religion accordingly. Ultimately, the rich aesthetic and theological tradition of the icons prevailed, and the church upheld its views of the union of divinity and humanity.

The continuing strength of the Orthodox church after these controversies shows in the expansion that followed. In the ninth century the Bulgars, a strong empire in the Balkans, embraced Eastern Christianity. In the later ninth and tenth centuries the rest of the Balkan nations, the Slavs, and finally Russia came into its orbit. Byzantine culture influenced that of Arabs to the East, transmitting knowledge of the Greek language and Greek philosophers, artistic styles, and techniques of work. The Mosque of Omar (Dome of the Rock), for example, built in Jerusalem in the late seventh century, has a Byzantine dome and Byzantine-style mosaics. In return, Byzantine artists learned from Arabic ornamental styles. We find in Orthodox Christianity from the seventh through the tenth centuries a religion united with a rich imperial culture, often at war with its Islamic neighbors but also participating in an exciting cultural exchange that helped the younger Islamic empires to mature and reach their own heights.

This great period gave way to another, more difficult one, however. The eleventh century brought internal difficulties, invasions by the Seljuk Turks and the Normans, and controversies with the West. Already a number of incidents had increased difficulties between East and West. In the sixth century the Latin church, combating Arians in Spain, had added a clause to its creed stating that the Holy Spirit proceeded from the Father "and the Son." This usage became entrenched in the church and was approved by Western authorities without ever being presented to a whole council of the church; the Greek branch had theological objections. In the ninth century, the rivalry between pope and partiarch had erupted into direct political conflict as Pope Nicholas I tried to intervene in the appointment of the Eastern patriarch.

Finally, in the eleventh century the Normans conquered the Byzantine colony of southern Italy, and Pope Leo IX insisted that the Orthodox change their allegiance from partiarch to pope. Naturally, the patriarch, Michael Cerularius, protested. In 1054 the pope sent three legates, headed by the strong-willed Bishop Humbert, to Constantinople to assert Western rights, but Cerularius received them scornfully. They then entered the cathedral of Saint Sophia and deposited there a bull of **excommunication** against Cerularius and his supporters. Michael immediately convoked a council and in return excommunicated the legates. This event has traditionally marked the formal division between Catholic and Orthodox churches, for despite later attempts to heal the breach, the two never reunited.

As we will see, the West later launched crusades that were intended in part to help the weakened East, suffering the attacks of the Turks. They accomplished nothing lasing in its defense, however, and the behavior of the crusaders and their eventual attack on

Constantinople itself destroyed relations between East and West. The disordered relations between the two branches weakened both civilizations when they had to face their enemies. The centuries of poor communication led to the West's losing touch with some of its original sources of spirituality, the great mystical and theological traditions of the East. On the other hand, the Eastern empire never recovered its strength after the onslaughts of Latin Christians and Muslims, and the Orthodox church, united as it was with its culture, suffered as well. Organizationally, the church divided into its various national branches—Greek, Russian, Serbian, Armenian, Syrian, and so on. The Russian church became so important that Moscow was given its own partiarch in the fourteenth century. These churches, however, regarded themselves as unified in tradition and never became competitive with one another as the later Western sects would be.

Moreover, the Eastern church continued its creativity in the realm of spirituality, especially in the centuries before the Turkish conquest of Constantinople (1453). The monks of the Byzantine empire developed a spiritual discipline known as "hesychasm," referring to the aim of the practice: tranquility or serenity. Their methods included specific postures and forms of breathing as well as mental concentration, similar in some respects to yogic or other forms of meditation. They repeated a prayer, usually the "Jesus Prayer" ("Lord Jesus Christ, Son of God, have mercy on me a sinner") as a kind of mantra, aiming to achieve a state of ceaseless prayer. This would ultimately result in a vision of God, not with the ordinary eye or even with the mind, but through divine illumination of one's being. This illumination by God's "grace" did not mean, as grace did in the West, that something was added to human nature, but rather that the human, the created being, now participated in God's uncreated "energies," that is, the powers that God manifests (his essence always remaining hidden). This was the mystical and theological development of the idea of deification, which as we noted before was prominent in Eastern thought and liturgy for centuries.

While the Eastern church developed its inward spirituality in theological reflection, continuing the imperial tradition, the Roman branch was developing the political allies it needed to ensure its survival. The pope sought the help of the Franks, who had converted to Christianity in 496 when their lord Clovis accepted baptism.

Their leaders afterwards helped Rome militarily against other societies (Arian Christian and pagan); and Rome sent, to both Gaul and England, Benedictine monks as missionaries and teachers. Irish monks also traveled into Frankish lands, and through these two sets of teachers Christianity began to penetrate Europe. After nearly two centuries of missionary work, however, many people had not accepted church discipline. A church council in 742 under the leadership of the great missionary Boniface ordered monks and priests to refrain from battle, insisted that priests give up their concubines, and forbade pagan rites such as animal sacrifices and magical incantations in the churches. Christianity was still competing with many older customs and religious practices.

A few decades later when Charles the Great (Charlemagne) took the throne, he renewed Boniface's orders and added other measures to strengthen the church. He ordered that all altars without relics be destroyed, that all oaths be sworn on a relic, and that no new saints be introduced. These steps aimed at orienting the clergy more firmly toward Rome, while at the same time insisting that Christianity alone was the guarantor of bonds between men. Further, Charles instituted a program of education, decreeing that every monastery and bishopric should set up a school. The prior state of learning is suggested by the fact that one Bavarian priest had been found baptizing converts *nomine patria et filia*, "in the name of the nation and the daughter," instead of the Father and the Son. Under the new system priests had to learn Latin, chanting, and calculation and had to memorize the major parts of the Mass and some sermons. Some would begin to study Scripture as well. At Charlemagne's encouragement books began to be collected and copied, and the Latin liturgy took definitive shape and spread through the realm.

Charlemagne's devotion to the faith and to Rome were recognized in his famous coronation in the year 800, when Pope Leo III anointed him Emperor of the Romans, creating what came to be known as the Holy Roman Empire. The coronation was a statement of Rome's independence from Constantinople, where there was already a Christian emperor. But it also officially confirmed that the Frankish rulers had accepted Christianity fully as an important dimension of their society. In 745 Pope Zacharias had written to the Frankish clergy and aristocrats, urging them to accept the reforms of Boniface. It was, he said, because they had false and misleading priests that their enemies had won battles. If the priests would become pure, observing chastity and refraining from bloodshed, the heathen would fall before the Christian armies. Christianity, in short, would provide the support of God for the Frankish warriors; they in turn would protect the church. Undoubtedly it had helped the cause that a Christian leader, Charles Martel, had won a great battle only a short time before, turning back the advance of the Muslim armies at Tours in 732. In any case, by 800 the coronation of Charles cemented the pact between church and state. Moreover, like the Eastern emperors, the Western ones came to believe they had a priestly role to fulfill: if the king, now emperor, fulfilled his obligations to God and dispensed justice and peace, he would ensure the salvation of his whole people. The bishops, on their part, believed it was their duty to keep the king and princes in line, advising them as to their Christian duties.

Nevertheless, the West could not duplicate the stability of the Eastern empire. By the late 800s Europe was again the target of raids from peoples on the perimeters. Vikings from Scandinavia, Magyars from Hungary, and Muslims in Spain engaged the people in continuous wars, reducing much of the population to dire poverty. Monks' chronicles tell of famines and epidemics, mob violence and mass deaths, even cannibalism in desperate attempts to stay alive. In this situation, power passed from the hands of the kings to the lesser nobles, each of whom built his own power base to fight the enemies, leading to a decentralized Europe and the social structure known as the feudal system. Power lay in the hands of the warrior class, the knights, who paid homage to their sire, the noble of a principality. This reorganization of European society marks the beginning of a new era following the general disorder of the previous centuries, after the fall of Rome and the gradual break with the East. But it was not, at first, an era in which the church could be confident of its strength.

The Western Middle Ages

Christianity in the eighth and ninth centuries had adjusted to being the religion of a warrior society, but it had firm attachments only at the higher levels of that society. The lesser nobles, who came to

The military orientation of early medieval Christianity in the West is suggested by these scenes from the Bayeaux Tapestry, about 1095, portraying events of the Norman conquest of England: William the Conqueror and his troops approaching the Mont St-Michel, and the English resisting the attack of the Norman Cavalry.

power in the debacle of the tenth-century invasions, did not always respect the traditional rights of the religious class as the anointed emperors had done. Struggles soon began between the lay aristocracy and the bishops and abbots of the church. Church councils made rules limiting the power of nobles, threatening them with excommunication if they did not obey. In the early eleventh century the church declared the "Peace of God" to forbid knights from destroying church property and killing unarmed peasants, monks, and priests. This was followed by the "Truce of God," which forbade the "joys of war" during Lent and urged Christians not to fight other Christians. Although many knights vowed to uphold these, the agreements did not succeed in controlling vendettas and the raids of armies.

Meanwhile, the nobles on their part were fighting back by simply appointing their own men to be bishops or abbots in their territory. Traditionally, a king consecrated to God's service could appoint a churchman by "investing" him with the symbols of his office—for example, ring, hat, and crozier for a bishop—but the church usually had a say in his election. The nobles, however, were taking this power into their hands with neither divine right nor church approval. In the late eleventh century a dispute of this sort disturbed all of Europe when Pope Gregory VII excommunicated one of the German kings, Henry IV, who was appointing his own church officials and opposing Gregory's reforms. Henry humbled himself before Gregory after a dramatic march through the snowy Alps—a wise political, as well as religious, move; Gregory had virtually no choice but to grant him forgiveness. After his return to Germany, however, Henry called a council of bishops that deposed Gregory from the papacy. The struggle, which came to be known as the investiture controversy, continued beyond the lifetimes of Henry and Gregory and was resolved only in 1122 at the Concordat of Worms, which set some limits on the power of church and state.

Despite the power of the lords, the church gradually gained political ground during the controversy. The religious punishments the church could use, its practical alliances, and the supportive system of bishops built by popes like Gregory yielded greater power than ever before. Moreover, Gregory's insistence on the independence of the church signaled the growing influence of a new movement in Europe: the monasteries of Cluny. Cluny had been founded in the tenth century by William the Pious, Duke of Aquitaine, under an unusual charter linking it to the saints Peter and Paul, and thus to Rome rather than to local powers, and permitting the monks to elect their own abbot without interference from duke or bishop. Cluny and the monasteries associated with it became famous for many things: their devotion to the life of prayer, their emphasis on music, and their encouragement of the great Romanesque architecture of the eleventh century.[3] But they also became centers of political power because of their fierce insistence on the independence of the church from secular control. Thus it is no accident that Gregory VII, educated at an Italian monastery influenced by Cluny, initiated an era of powerful popes.

The investiture controversy was only one aspect of a new spirit in the church that, we can see in retrospect, was preparing the ground for a new religious movement. By the last twenty years of the eleventh century Christian ideals and expectations had permeated most of European society; the reputation of Cluny was setting a model of discipline and devotion; and the knights, who sought to participate in Christian society but whose lust for battle often burst the bounds of Christian discipline, had become a powerful class. The fuel was ready. The spark was lit in a dramatic address by Pope Urban II, speaking to a public session at the end of a council of bishops meeting in 1095 at Clermont, France. Urban appealed to those present to come to the aid of the Eastern church, which was suffering at the hands of its Muslim conquerors. He also sought aid for Jerusalem, appealing to his listeners' fascination with the holy sepulcher of Christ and assuring them that any who died in battle would be forgiven their sins. Thus Urban launched the First Crusade.

Popular response was overwhelming. Soon nobles were leading armies of trained soldiers while popular visionaries led thousands of poorer men, and even bands of children, toward Constantinople and Jerusalem. Defeating "the infidel" became the watchword of Europe. Mobs began massacring Jews, especially in the Rhineland, where more Jews were killed than in Jerusalem. The peasants' branch of the movement, known as the People's Crusade, arrived disorderly and hungry in Constantinople in 1096. The Eastern emperor, shocked at the sort of help sent by the West, provided them with rations, but most soon met death in Asia Minor in battles with the Muslims. The serious armies, arriving a few months later, spent time arguing with the emperor but eventually went on and, after lengthy battles, captured Jerusalem in 1099. As a result, several small Christian states existed in the region for nearly a hundred years, until the Muslims retook Jerusalem in 1187. Succeeding crusades failed to establish any significant expansion of Christian power. Meanwhile, the professed goal of the Crusades, to help the Eastern church, had disappeared. In 1204, during the Fourth Crusade, Western warriors attacked Constantinople itself, incurring the wrath of the East.

The spiritual revival that the West experienced in the eleventh century with the growth of Cluny, the reforms of Gregory, and the First Crusade came to fruit in the next several generations. The twelfth century has been called a time of renaissance, a proto-Reformation, or the beginning of modernity; and the thirteenth is generally considered the peak of medieval civilization. The components of these developments were numerous: the growth of learning in monasteries and cathedral schools; the first universities; greater church involvement in secular affairs; an upsurge of religious devotion, especially to the Virgin and the Eucharist, and an increase in pilgrimage; the rise of heresies and the establishment of the **Inquisition**; new monastic orders, the Franciscans and the Dominicans; the rise of mysticism; and a revolution in art that culminated in the Gothic cathedral. Throughout, we can see significant changes in the way people regarded the divine or spiritual realm in relation to the human or material. In this period humanity and materiality took on a higher value, and gradually people came to see holiness within the world as well as coming from outside it.

One of the clearest examples of this transformation was the new work in the world of the intellect. In the eleventh century scholars began to re-examine Christian faith, seeking to understand it in terms of human reason. This was the beginning of the movement known as scholasticism. After 1085, when Spanish Christians conquered Muslim Toledo, Christians with the help of multilingual Jewish scholars began retranslating into Latin the Arabic translations of ancient Greek philosophers, the most important being Aristotle. Scholars flocked to Toledo and brought back the manuscripts that would further transform Christian theology. Intellectual life began to move out of the monasteries and into the universities at Paris, Oxford, and elsewhere. In the monasteries, study had been preliminary to prayer, *lectio* (reading) merely a preparation for *contemplatio*, the soul's search for God. The universities began to take a different turn, valuing learning as a means of gaining clarity and understanding in one's approach to God and allowing learning to be sought for its own sake. Further, the new **friars**, Franciscans and Dominicans, who contributed much to the growth of learning, were also more involved in the world. An interest in human knowledge and the capacities of the human mind struck new chords in the twelfth century and afterward.

These developments came to fruition in the thirteenth century in the work of the greatest medieval theologian, also a popular teacher, the Dominican Thomas Aquinas (1225–1274). Aquinas came to the fore in the Aristotelian controversy, as Greek philosophy was being introduced into university curricula. Some thinkers influenced by the Greeks were proposing radical ideas, such as that all human minds were but parts of one great Mind, or that the world was eternal. Others feared such ideas might undermine the church, calling into question the doctrine that God was a personal deity, or that God created the world from nothing and would bring it to an end. As a result certain propositions related to Aristotle's thought were condemned in the 1270s. Thomas Aquinas, however, developed a form of Aristotelianism that was acceptable to the church. His *Summa Theologica* ("comprehensive theology"), though still incomplete when he died, continued to attract other theologians and provided the foundation for Roman Catholic theology down to the twentieth century.

Thomas diverged from Augustine, the rock of Christian thought since the fifth century. Augustine had emphasized the dependence of human beings on God: by God's grace, the human will is enabled to do good; by his divine illumination, the human mind is enabled to reach truth. The purely human side—the body, the senses, the ordinary mind—is at best only a vehicle, not a source, of good or truth; at worst, it is an obstacle. Aquinas rejected Augustine's dualism and held, in harmony with Aristotle, that the spiritual and the material were related rather than opposed. True knowledge begins not with divine illumination but with basic sensory experience of the world, followed by reflection using the natural faculty of human reason. Through this process one arrives at knowledge of "universals"—what we might call ultimate concepts as to the essences of things—which, as with Augustine, were the supreme truths.

This theory had important ramifications: human reason, and indeed human nature generally, were in the image of God. They were flawed by sin but not, as Augustine had held, completely corrupted.

Humans needed correction by God's grace, mediated by the sacraments as medicine mediates healing power. Once corrected, human faculties could achieve perfection and human souls reach their true goal of full likeness to God. God's grace, in short, enabled human efforts to cooperate in God's own divine activity: to bring all souls to himself. The material and the spiritual, the natural and the supernatural, reason and revelation, were intertwined in a grand system that existed in perfection in the mind of God.

This was radical thinking in the thirteenth century, but it was paralleled in many ways by the intertwining of the religious and secular worlds in practical action. As we have seen, papal power was growing in the late eleventh and twelfth centuries. As intellectual life became more important, the church's control of education meant greater social power. The church drew on a centralized and dependable source of wealth, the papal treasury, and possessed an efficient bureaucracy. By the early thirteenth century, Pope Innocent III— who once wroted privately of himself that he was "less than God but more than man"—could influence the politics of all Europe. By frequent use of interdictions to suspend masses and other church rites in a given region he brought German, French, and English princes into submission to the church. He called the great Fourth Lateran Council in 1215, which became a significant event in unifying the church. He supported and integrated into the church the new Franciscan and Dominican orders, thus bringing many potential dissidents into the mainstream, while also centralizing the Inquisition (introduced in the late twelfth century) to deal summarily with others. Innocent's rule was the peak of papal power, and it indicated how human and spiritual power were joining forces in the Middle Ages.

The changes among the elite in thought and politics found a reflection in forms of religious expression among the laity. New monastic orders, lay organizations, or heretical groups appeared in almost every generation from 1100 to 1300. Within the mainstream of the church, lay confraternities devoted to the Eucharist emerged in the twelfth century, emphasizing the importance of **communion** and glorifying the moment of the **elevation of the host**, when the priest raised the bread for all to see. Innocent III officially declared the doctrine of **transubstantiation** (long an accepted church tradition): the wafer of bread and the wine actually became, in substance,

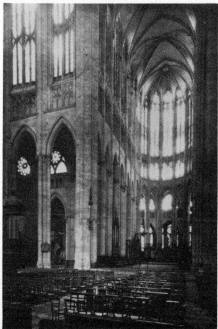

The artistic achievements of the western Middle Ages culminated in the Gothic cathedral with its strong architectural construction, detailed sculptural design, stained glass windows, and effective use of interior light. Here are shown (1) Amiens Cathedral, France, built 1220–1288 (except for the towers, 1366–1420). Photo used by permission of G. E. Kidder Smith, New York. (2) The interior of Beauvais Cathedral, France (begun 1247). Used by permission of Kresge Photo Study Archive, Department of Art, Oberlin College.

the body and blood of Christ. This was a shift from the attitude of
the ninth and tenth centuries, when the Eucharist was regarded as
more like a relic of Christ. Now the accent was on the transformation of ordinary material into the substance of Christ himself.

The same period also saw a striking increase in expressions of
devotion to the Virgin Mary, mother of Jesus. Previously local and
regional saints and their relics had dominated popular devotion.
Now there appeared numerous popular prayers to Mary (notably
the Ave Maria), stories of her miracles, and portrayals of the Virgin
in painting and statuary. Innocent III officially endorsed, despite the
opposition of many scholastic philosophers, the popular feasts celebrating the **Immaculate Conception** of Mary (when she herself
was conceived without **original sin**). The movement of devotion
centering around Mary was epitomized by the sermons of Bernard
of Clairvaux, a leading figure of the twelfth century and a great mystic who organized a new monastic order (the Cistercians) and
preached the Second Crusade. He urged all who were troubled to
turn to Mary, to call out to Mary, in every kind of danger or hard-
ship, for she was the guiding star for human life. Bernard and others
gave impetus to the great movement of Marian piety that has continued in Roman Catholicism down to the present. It represented
another re-evaluation of the human world, specifically, of the feminine elements that, except for a few local female saints, had been
ignored for centuries. The Virgin was the perfect woman, through
whom one could approach Christ the king. That a woman should
be so exalted was significant, when a few centuries earlier monks
had debated whether women even had souls. Mary was unique,
however, for she was chaste and sinless, unlike ordinary women who
were tainted by the sin of sexuality like the first woman, Eve.
"Alone of all her sex" as the phrase went, she could be glorified and
venerated. Even with this qualification, however, the cult of Mary
represented a shift in attitudes toward women and the feminine.
Soon to follow was the more secular code of chivalry, glorifying the
pure woman as the lady of love to whom every knight should bow
and whose love was the most desired of all goals.

We have already mentioned briefly the new orders of friars, the
Franciscans and Dominicans. Their members were not cloistered
(i.e., confined to monasteries) but preached in the towns. Dom-
inic (1170–1221) saw his followers as primarily a teaching and

preaching order, bringing religious knowledge to people while also battling the heretics. Francis (1182–1226) was more radical. He insisted on apostolic poverty—owning nothing, relying on no one but God for support—as the foundation of spirituality and taught his followers to travel about teaching, praying, and helping those in need. Church leaders were concerned about the potentially disruptive character of a movement that insisted that true followers of Christ should possess no property; thus a later leader, Bonaventura, who headed the order from 1257 to 1274, adjusted the ideals of poverty and itineracy to make the Franciscans more like the other monastic orders.

Other more marginal groups flourished as well. The Spiritual Franciscans, who wanted to keep Francis's original ideals, broke off from the main body and took up the ideas of an earlier mystical philosopher, Joachim of Fiore, who had taught that the age of the Father and the Son had passed and a new age of the Holy Spirit had arrived. The church promptly declared them heretics. A laywomen's movement emerged in the cities of France, the Netherlands, and the Rhineland: the Beguines, who dedicated themselves to a life of higher spirituality together with work in the world. One of the great Christian heresies flourished in southern France in this period, namely, Catharism, which adopted Gnostic ideas of extreme dualism, denying the goodness of the material world. These ideas had spread from the East, most recently from a teacher named Bogomil in the Bulgar empire, where the Eastern church had been fighting such groups for centuries. The Cathars believed that the elect could subdue the body by perfecting the spirit, not in itself an unusual idea. But they were heretics because they rejected the sacraments and practiced only the laying on of hands; moreover, they allowed women to act as priests. (Since the body was evil, however, procreation was discouraged, and pregnant women were denied the laying on of hands.) The orthodox church acted vigorously to stamp out the Cathars by means of the papal Inquisition; still, it took nearly two centuries before their churches were effectively undermined.

As the church was becoming more worldly, such heresies as the Cathars offered an alternative, more otherworldly in orientation. So too did another movement within the church, namely, that of mysticism. Mysticism was not truly a popular movement, for only a few rare individuals were mystics; nevertheless, it indicated a far-reaching interest in the interior life. Mystics adopted a more intense discipline in order to gain a direct experience of spiritual reality, ideally a vision of God. Their approaches differed considerably depending on their tradition and their own experience. Yet we may take as an example the approach developed by Bernard of Clairvaux.

Bernard taught that the spiritual life progresses by stages developed through disciplined control of one's action and prayerful devotion to God. He set them forth as follows: compunction, devotion, repentance, good words and prayer, contemplation, and love. Compunction meant recognizing one's evil ways followed by cutting away one's bad habits. Devotion was the first joyful turning to God, hoping for pardon. Repentance included fasting, keeping nighttime vigils, and other difficult tasks, while good works and prayer sustained the soul. Contemplation was like a dream of God, beholding him as though in polished metal, but not yet face to face. Love was the perfection of the heart that warmed the soul. If one followed the stages faithfully, one could, over the years, come to a vivid and powerful experience of the love of God, which Bernard regarded as the ultimate attainment. Other mystics defined the stages slightly differently or described the goal in a different fashion—for example, as the union with God in knowledge of God. All, however, were turning away from involvement in events of the day toward a more intense experience of the inner life. Their creativity contributed another dimension to the rich culture of the High Middle Ages.

In theology, in politics, in popular devotion, and in the search for higher spirituality these centuries were an enormously creative period. We should not imagine, however, that they were also a time of freedom or tolerance in our modern sense. The church, and most European Christians, remained on the defensive in regard to outsiders or those of divergent beliefs and practices. The Inquisition was on the alert for heresy; Abelard, a recognized scholar, was declared a heretic, and a great mystic, Meister Eckhart of Germany, was accused of heresy. The church hierarchy regarded many of Francis's ideas as highly questionable. Moreover, this was the period in which perceptions of the Jews began to change: instead of regarding them as resident aliens, accepted although not necesssarily possessing the same rights as others, Christians began seeing them as the demonic infidels within the walls of Christendom itself (as Muslims were the infidels outside). Attacks on Jews during the Crusades were part of this pattern. So were expulsions: in 1290 Jews were expelled from England, in 1305 from France, in 1492 and 1497 from Spain and Portugal, respectively. Intolerance and a fear of difference were part of the triumph of Christian culture in Europe.

European Religious Reformation

The gradual growth of lay devotional movements, mysticism, and dissidence reflected some dissatisfaction with traditional authority and a desire to modify religious practices in the Roman Catholic church. Although scholastic theology continued to be developed and refined throughout the fourteenth and fifteenth centuries, radical leaders began to challenge common practices of the church. In the late fourteenth century an English writer, John Wycliffe, called for vernacular translations of the Bible, lay communion with both bread and wine, the right of secular courts to punish clergy, and an end to the sale of indulgences. A group that took up his ideas, the Lollards, was implicated in uprisings against the crown a few years later. In Bohemia, John Huss of the University of Prague led a related movement based on Wycliffe's ideas, with the result that the Czech armies threatened to invade other parts of Europe. The Council of Basel in 1449 settled that particular dispute, but these movements foreshadowed the growth of large popular, sometimes nationalistic, movements for religious reform.

The conditions leading to the call for reform were manifold. Europe suffered a great deal of inner turmoil in the fourteenth and early fifteenth centuries. The Black Death beginning in 1348 destroyed one-third of Europe's population. The Hundred Years' War, a series of conflicts between England and France (1337–1453), directed a great deal of energy into military ventures. The church hierarchy became caught up in its own controversies and enmeshed in international politics. The papacy had tied itself to France and moved to Avignon from 1309 to 1377. At the end of this period, the **cardinals**, divided between French and Italian sympathies, elected one pope in April 1377, then another in September. This, the Great Western Schism in the papacy, persisted through the reigns of several popes, and a complication was added when the

The Renaissance saw a new humanizing of art and religion, as exemplified in Michelangelo's famous paintings on the ceiling of the Sistine Chapel (1508–1512). This scene, depicting "The Creation of Adam," shows even God in anthropomorphic form, and the human body is portrayed in its full glory. Used by permission of SCALA/Art Resource, New York.

Council of Pisa declared both popes heretical and elected a third. Not until the Council of Constance (1414–17) was the schism healed. Such difficulties in the papacy, supposedly the central axis of Christendom, signified a profound unsettlement in all of Europe. Meanwhile, the beginnings of the Renaissance suggested new visions of humanity in art and literature. The recovery of interest in the human form, in human emotions, and in the various disciplines of human reason—often modeled on the culture of ancient Greece—were a source of inspiration and a challenge to medieval traditions.

The late fourteenth and fifteenth centuries were also an age of proliferation of religious observances, to the point that they became easy targets of criticism. Pilgrimages, devotions to the saints, and religious processions on holy days were important to the laity as religious expressions over which they had a great deal of control. But the learned accused them of being less matters of spiritual discipline and sacrifice than social occasions. Also, the endowment of masses had reached enormous proportions. Since ancient times it had been common to endow masses to be said after one's own death or the death of a relative for the repose of the soul; the funds went to the proper support of priests. But now the number of masses had increased unreasonably. In 1244 at Durham, England, the monks were supposed to say 7,332 masses a year. Henry VIII in the sixteenth century was said to have bought twelve thousand masses at sixpence apiece. The sense of proportion between spiritual exercises and monetary support was being lost in a changing economy, in which money was becoming increasingly the measure of value.

There were similar problems with indulgences, problems that generated much controversy. An indulgence was a papal decree that granted a person remission from punishment in **purgatory** for his or her sins. (It did not grant forgiveness, which came only from the sacrament of **penance**.) Originally indulgences might be granted in return for a spiritual service, as when Urban II promised indulgences to crusaders in 1095. By the fifteenth century, however, one could, at least unofficially, buy an indulgence for money, and other corruptions had ensued—as in 1476 when Pope Sixtus IV allowed people to obtain indulgences for their dead relatives suffering in purgatory. Buying and selling of church offices (the sin of simony) had increased, and many priests and bishops were known to be living with concubines. In some cases they were absolved of their sins on payment of fees—concubinage fees, "cradle fees" for illegitimate children, and the like. This naturally led to mistrust between people and priest. Though laypeople did not neglect the sacraments, they sometimes turned to itinerant priests who seemed more holy than their own parish leaders, and they continued to seek alternative forms of devotion.

In the late fifteenth and sixteenth centuries a number of learned men issued serious criticisms of the church. A Dominican friar in Florence named Savonarola attacked corruption, gathered a large following, and prophesied a millennial upheaval that would bring thorough reform. Erasmus, one of the great Catholic humanists, wrote treatises expounding the need for reform and aimed humorous jabs at the church. Martin Luther, a friar and professor at the University of Wittenberg, had a distinctive religious experience that led him to reformulate the doctrine of **justification** and sharply criticize the church for its practices. Ignatius of Loyola, following his own inner experience, developed a kind of meditation that disciplined the will to obedience. Luther's preaching and writing sparked the Protestant Reformation and marked the beginning of the Lutheran church. Ignatius founded the highly disciplined and dedicated order, the Society of Jesus (Jesuits), whose teaching and missions deeply affected the Roman Catholic church. The religious scene in Europe would never be the same after the sixteenth-century reformers.

The changes came most dramatically and quickly in the areas that became Protestant, notably Germany and Switzerland. There the burghers—the lay citizens, nonaristocrats—had been gaining power for a century. Whenever possible, they had taxed church lands and tried to insist that clergy be part of the citizenry, not a separate estate. They had endowed preacherships for themselves to satisfy their need for learning. Much of Luther's support came from among these lay-endowed preachers. Thus, from the beginning Protestantism represented a new and strong option for the laity that was not just a weaker version of the ascetic piety of the monks. The Reformers upheld the religiousness of the layperson who was involved in the ordinary world of work, money, and sexuality.

The first Reformers, led by Luther in Germany and by Ulrich Zwingli and then John Calvin in Switzerland, attacked the monastic ideal first of all. Whereas the monastic life created a separate state of holiness, Protestant thinkers emphasized that every profession was a "calling," not just the religious professions. Another important tenet was the "priesthood of all believers," meaning that every Christian was in charge of his or her relation to God without the mediation of a priest. Especially was this true of penance (as well as extreme unction, a form of penance for the dying), which most Protestant preachers attacked. By the fifteenth century penance had become a lengthy proving of the individual, as the confessor checked off long lists of major and minor sins. Protestants regarded this as improper both because it made the person dependent on the confessor and because it required the impossible feat of perfect memory and full knowledge of all possible sins. They argued instead that any Christian could confess to any other; all believers were in this sense "priests."

Protestants went on to do away with a number of important practices. The sacraments of penance and extreme unction were eliminated, as was the taking of monastic vows. Marriage and **confirmation** were no longer regarded as sacraments, nor was a priest's or a minister's **ordination**. Supplementary penitential practices like the endowment of masses or the making of pilgrimages also disappeared. Baptism and the Eucharist remained, and different Protestants disagreed over the nature of each. Though most churches still baptized infants, some more radical reformers limited baptism to adults. As to the Eucharist, the Protestants did away with the multiplicity of masses and substituted an occasional celebration of the Lord's Supper. Some Reformers, like Luther, continued to hold that Christ's body was present in the Eucharist; others, like Zwingli, saw the Supper as a memorial only. In either case, the significance of the Mass tended to diminish among most Protestants.

The substitute for the sacraments in virtually all Protestant churches was the preaching of "the Word," that is, the holy scriptures, and the reception of that word by the believer, in faith. Luther's central new doctrine, the cornerstone of all Reformers, was "justification through grace by faith alone." One became righteous in the eyes of God, not by any external works, whether the Eucharist itself or penitential pilgrimages, but only by one's faith in the saving acts of Jesus Christ. The preaching of the word according to Scripture was the means provided for arousing faith. Thus *sola fide, sola scriptura*—by faith alone, by Scripture alone—became slogans of the Protestant movement. In addition most Protestant thinkers held that Christians were so totally dependent on God that they could do nothing to create faith in themselves. God had predestined each soul to salvation (Calvin held that he had also predestined some to be damned). Thus the Reformation emphasized, in the style of Augustine, the direct sovereignty of God over the soul, the Christian's own responsibility for his or her relation to God, and the church as a vehicle of the Word by which faith was awakened and brought to maturity.

The Reformation spread quickly in Germany and Switzerland, though a number of areas remained Catholic (and political alliances played a considerable part in religious allegiances). In France the Huguenots represented a strong Protestant force at first but in the late sixteenth century experienced severe persecution. In England the Reformation began from royal initiative, when Henry VIII broke

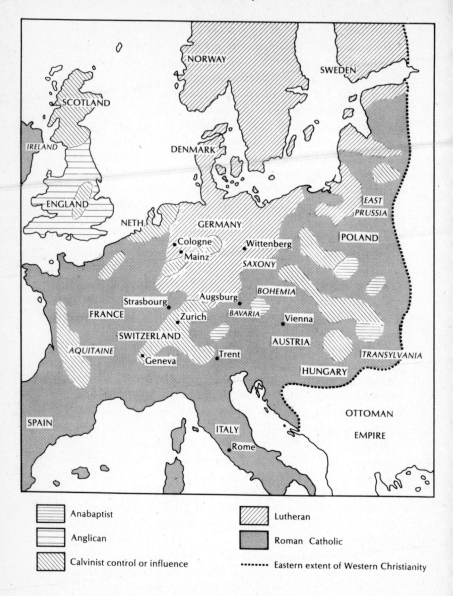

Anabaptist

Anglican

Calvinist control or influence

Lutheran

Roman Catholic

.... Eastern extent of Western Christianity

Divisions of European Christianity after the Reformation

with the pope because he could not get his latest marriage annulled. Though the next ruler, Mary, was Catholic, Elizabeth followed and, from 1559 on, promoted a gradual Reformation that created the Church of England (later to be named, in the United States, the Episcopal Church).

Many of the larger denominations of today came from the main branches of early Protestantism. Lutheran churches came from Luther's protest; the Reformed churches (German, Dutch, etc.) from the combined work of Calvin and Zwingli. Calvinism traveled to England and blended with other elements to become Puritanism, a movement attempting to "purify" the Church of England. From this came Presbyterian, Congregationalist, Baptist, and Quaker groups. A later reform of the Church of England produced, in the eighteenth century, the Methodist church. Of these, the Baptists and Quakers were the most radical. They were akin to another stream of reform, today called the Radical Reformation, that is less well known—the groups it produced tended to be small and independent—but equally important.

The radical Reformers held that the church should become perfect—according to some, by returning to the ideals of primitiveChristianity, according to others, by following the immediate guidance of the Holy Spirit. Abolishing the monastic life and certain other rituals and doctrines was not sufficient. Most of the radicals insisted that the church should contain only voluntary believers, that is, those who joined as adults. Some therefore rebaptized their members (who had already received baptism as infants) and earned the name Anabaptists, or "baptized again." This practice especially aroused the furor not only of Catholics but also of mainstream Reformers, for it suggested that all their churches were wrongly constituted. Some radicals were pacifists; others—early Baptists, Quakers, Mennonites—refused to be involved in secular government at all; still others were willing to use force to revolutionize society. Some groups were quiet and contemplative, emphasizing the inner work of the Holy Spirit within the believer—the Quakers are the best known example. Many believed that the millennium would arrive at any moment, with the Second Coming of Christ; that was why it was important to separate from the world and create the perfect Christian church and society.

What united most of the radicals was their insistence on the freedom of the church from state interference. They believed that Catholicism had allowed the system of authority to be corrupted by entanglement in secular politics. In the Protestant Reformation as well, the new religious principles seemed to be gaining a foothold not because of purity of faith but by alliance with magistrates, town councils, or princes. The few who wanted to revolutionize society wanted only the saints to rule. In short, the radicals wanted no secular authority to have any influence over the religious life. Their unwillingness to compromise on this point preserved their autonomy as self-governing religious groups, but it also decreased their social power. They simply could not command the influence that the larger Reformation possessed.

Meanwhile, however, Roman Catholic rulers in France, Spain, Austria, and the small states of Italy disliked all these Reformations. Remembering the Hussite rebellion of the last century, they wanted to set their own house in order, create peace and unity among Catholics, and win back some of the ground they had lost to the new "heretics." Therefore the church called a great convocation, the Council of Trent, which met in three long sessions spanning the years from 1545 to 1563.

Trent represented a long process of coming to agreement in an age of confusion when many former certainties had become questionable. Later historians have often accused the council of being extremely conservative, simply restating old views. Such a judgment is not fair, however. The theologians and bishops who gathered at Trent spent hundreds of hours re-examining old statements and hammering out the Roman Catholic doctrines of original sin, of justification, and of the sacraments. Those in attendance often held diverse views. If some of the statements sounded traditional or conservative, that is because, first, the best Catholic minds of the age held them to be still correct and, second, those in attendance valued the unity of the church over their private divergent views. One cardinal refused to state his views of justification in public. It was later discovered that he agreed essentially with Luther, but he did not wish to contribute to the troubles of the church; therefore, he kept silent and submitted to whatever the council, as the agent of God's Spirit, would decide.

Ultimately, the Council of Trent offered important statements of doctrine that, though not substantially new, now clearly formulated what was to be taught. The council added a new emphasis on teaching: it provided for the education of the lower clergy in institutions called seminaries and encouraged the wider teaching of the **catechism**. Under Ignatius of Loyola's new order, the Society of Jesus, the missionary work of education would be carried out with great vigor. The Jesuits were largely responsible for returning Poland to the Catholic fold, as well as for the conversion of many Native Americans to the Catholic faith.

Further, the council reformed the structure of the church, giving the bishops greater responsibility for what happened in their domains and urging them to reside permanently in their sees. A large number of the council believed that the difficulties in the church were due, not to wrong doctrine or practice, but to the fact that bishops and priests had become distant from their communities; they were no longer bringing to them the "bread of the gospel" and showing its power by their own holy lives. The Jesuit theologian Alphonsus Salmeron preached to the council that priests and bishops had come to desire honor and fear rather than love from their parishioners, that they were seeking mainly to satisfy their ambitions rather than to be "good shepherds" like Christ. Salmeron's sentiment was widely shared. Therefore the spirit of Trent moved to reinstate the authorities of the church but with a renewed concern for, and a genuine relationship to, those under their authority. By clarifying the responsibilities of the various levels of the hierarchy, the council did what it could to encourage that development.

The Roman Catholic reforms aimed to build up the church, to strengthen it at the core. So, too, the Protestants wanted a strong and healthy Christian church. The differences in their approaches, however, were crucial. The Catholics saw the church's core as being the ordained priests and bishops, those who held the power of the sacraments; if they were set on the right path the church would regain its health. The Protestants radically revalued the religious life of the laity, asserting that they represented the strength of the church. They therefore diminished the importance of special callings (like the priesthood and the monastic orders) and the sacramental life (which depended on priests). Instead, they emphasized the faith of the believer, which was a matter between the individual and God. In the Radical Reformation this emphasis on the inner life was sometimes exalted to a total dependence on the workings of the

Holy Spirit. In the mainstream, however, the role of the church remained important: the church was the vehicle of the saving Word. Only through the church and its messengers, the preachers, could one have knowledge of Scripture and the basic gospel message that, in turn, could awaken faith. The ministry was therefore a special calling, but it was no longer set apart as especially holy. All vocations were callings, and all citizens could respect one another and provide mutual support within the church and society. The various views that emerged in the Reformation era represented different visions of society and of the church as an organic body; these would continue to shape the nature of each church through the following centuries.

Orthodox churches in Poland, Russia, the Balkans, and Greece were much less affected by these reform movements. Some local councils, to define the essentials of faith, developed "confessions" on the Protestant model, but these never achieved wide acceptance. The conflicts that fueled the western Reformation—between church and state, between clergy and laity—were less pressing in the orthodox churches where the liturgy and the worshiping community continued to be the focus of unity.

New Worlds

In the meantime the era of the religious revivals known as Reformation and Counter-Reformation also saw one of the most revolutionary events in world history: European (re-)discovery and settlement of the American continents. Columbus and the seamen who followed him discovered eventually a way around the world, and set the stage for a new era in Christianity. Beginning in the sixteenth century and continuing down to the present, missionaries transported Christian doctrine and practice to the Americas, southern Africa, Asia, Australia, and the Pacific islands. At the same time the Russian Orthodox church sent missions to Asia, Japan, and Alaska. Each region contributed to the variety of Christian life, for each culture added its imprint to the underlying structure of Catholic or Protestant faith. The resulting forms of Christianity ranged from direct transplants of European churches to fascinating amalgams of native and European religions, to new reform movements under the leadership of native prophets. It is impossible to survey them all; nevertheless it will be instructive to look at some of the contrasting styles and results just on the American continents.

In Mexico, for one example, Spanish Catholic missionaries (Jesuits, Dominicans, and Franciscans) encountered a highly civilized society that had been ruled by the Aztecs. The friars clearly held their own religion to be superior and accused the Mexicans of idol worship, but they also recognized in the native religion similarities to Christian or biblical practices. Some argued that Aztec religion was a degenerate form of a superior religion, that perhaps one of the apostles—mostly likely Thomas—had brought the gospel to Mexico, but after his death the truth had been lost and the Christian message corrupted. Mexicans sometimes identified Saint Thomas with Quetzalcoatl, a former king/god who was expected to return at the end of time. Similarly, the great goddess Tonantzin was translated into the Virgin Mary and became Our Lady of Guadalupe, later a symbol of Mexican nationalism. Thus in certain societies where Spanish Catholicism met a strong native religion, a kind of syncretism developed wherein new holy figures and new practices were superimposed on the local beliefs.

However, not all missionaries were so open or so tolerant as to allow old beliefs and practices to continue. Especially when in contact with Native American societies that they regarded as primitive, missionaries declared the people of these societies to be ignorant and depraved, with customs that were totally immoral. In such situations, Catholics and Protestants alike viewed their task as bringing civilization and Christianity to lands and people barren of human virtue. Still, the Catholic approach differed from the Protestant. The Spanish Catholics who ruled most parts of the Americas held to their religion and intermarried with the local inhabitants; the missionaries meanwhile instructed the people to a level at which they knew the catechism and had begun to move away from their former "superstitions." If possible, they tried to gather them into Spanish-style villages and towns where they would learn European ways more quickly. Over the generations the gradualist approach and intermarriage with Europeans created a hierarchical society of mixed ethnicities. Catholicism, the religion of the conquerors, became the religion of high-status citizens, thus unifying the church across national lines and adding to its wealth and power. Also, the church often saw itself as protector of the poor, trying to bring the lower classes and even the enslaved into the church. Nevertheless, Catholic attitudes were not uniform. In non-Spanish areas, such as French Canada and Louisiana, Catholics were tolerant of local traditions, but less open to intermarriage. Thus, a variety of Catholic societies developed in the New World.

The English Protestant colonies, most of which eventually became part of the United States, differed sharply in their pattern. Immigration styles were different: not friars and soldiers, explorers and traders (the latter often looking for female partners), but family groups focused on farming and village life. Protestants usually objected to intermarriage, viewing Native Americans and African slaves in a harsher light than did the Catholics. At first, very few settlers cared about the conversion of the Indians or of the black slaves. Moreover, Protestantism offered little of the ritual life or rich store of legends of the saints that could more easily integrate people from traditional societies into their communities. The Protestant missionary expected converts to learn to speak and read English, read Scripture, and attend a church highly focused on the verbal— indeed, centered on a long and complex sermon. A few members of the eastern tribes did assimilate into Protestant societies, but soon Indian wars took priority over Indian missions. When territorial expansion began after the American Revolution, relations were marked by wars and oft-broken treaties. Missionaries carried on their work, but only a few strong native churches emerged until after the Indians had been forced onto reservations, in the late nineteenth century.

Other difficulties arose in Christians' relations to African slaves. In South America Africans were generally regarded as the lowest class; yet the possibility of intermarriage meant gradual change through the generations. In the Anglo-American world, however, slaveowners generally did not recognize their children by black concubines, and all blacks remained at the level of slaves. The slaves had come for the most part from the highly developed civilizations of West Africa. Yet, separated from their families and countrymen, they soon lost touch with the richness of their home cultures. Nor did slaveowners make strong efforts to integrate them into Christian culture. After the eighteenth-century religious **revivals** (to be discussed later), some slaveowners began instructing their slaves in the rudiments of Christianity, but in the nineteenth century slaveowners discouraged education for slaves, for they feared that teaching them to read the Bible might lead them to revolt. As a result, black American Christianity took a form different from Native American, Protestant, or Catholic Christianity. Thanks to their ancient African heritage, blacks retained a preference for ecstatic religion, dance, body movement, and responsive chanting that still characterize some black churches. On the American scene, their religion developed primarily in the age of revivals, so it was highly evangelical; since masters discouraged education, they relied on oral tradition, song, and dramatic preaching styles. The result is a unique form of Christianity that only in recent times has begun to be recognized in its full richness.

Modern Developments in Christianity

Amid the diversity that grew out of worldwide Christian missions, there were some additional developments that affected virtually all forms of Christianity. These stem largely from the religious awakenings of the eighteenth century and later, usually called revivals. The United States, England, and Germany have been the primary sites for these awakenings, although most other Christian countries have been touched in some ways.

In the seventeenth century the United States and most European countries had settled into the church divisions already mentioned, coming from the mainstream and the radical reformations. In the United States many denominations were represented; however, the dominant tradition was Puritanism, deeply rooted in New England culture and expressed through the Congregational and Presbyterian churches. Highly intellectual, yet deeply concerned about the individual's inner development in faith, the Puritan tradition maintained itself through a strong vision of the church as the center of society. In England the Church of England held a similar position, threatened only by the Puritan dissenters, who wanted to place their churches in the center. In Germany the Lutherans dominated. By the middle of the eighteenth century, however, in all three areas a movement developed that encouraged greater inward devotion, greater individual piety. Sometimes adherents formed a new sect;

the Methodists, led by John Wesley, eventually were forced to break off from the Church of England, but in the Lutheran church, the Pietists were accepted without having to make a break.

The primary significance of this movement, however, was that it opened the way toward a greater role for emotions in Christian faith. Protestants, with their emphasis on the inward faith of the believer, and Catholics, with their strong mystical tradition, had always recognized that emotions had a place in Christian experience. The American Puritans had greatly developed their sensitivity in that direction, shaping their religious lives in an inward quest for peace, over against the continual Calvinist uncertainty about salvation. The question, Was I predestined to be one of the elect? created a dynamic of anxiety, terror, and hope that became a hallmark of Puritanism. But in the eighteenth century these and other emotions began to emerge into the open. They were no longer a matter merely of private communication between the individual and God but were visibly expressed in response to a minister's sermon. Great preachers like Jonathan Edwards, America's first original theologian, were startled to find their audiences deeply and openly affected, and then rather quickly converted to a profound love of Christ. Less publicly, the small circles of believers who were Methodists in England or Pietists in Germany shared their inner religious feelings and supported one another in developing a deeper Christian experience.

These beginnings heralded the emergence of a different type of Christianity, known often as revivalistic or, more broadly, evangelical. More properly, we should regard it as experiential (in the late eighteenth century the term would have been "experimental") Christianity: a form of religious expression in which the believer's personal experience, testimony to that experience, and heartfelt expression of it in prayer or song became central. In the eighteenth century, these expressions were still largely contained within the orderly forms of the church, supplemented by prayer fellowships or an occasional extra meeting. In the nineteenth century, however, they exploded into a long era of revivals. Frontier revivals, known for their wild ecstasies; annual church revivals, in which the regular congregation gathered for an extra series of meetings; mass revivals in the larger towns and cities: all these were popular variations on a single theme, the religion of inward experience. Along with offering personal prayers aloud and sharing experience with others came a great rush of hymn writing by laypeople (in Britain and the United States, by large numbers of women). The "gospel hymn" (of the white middle-class culture, not the black) became the theme song of the new era. In modern times the great mass revivalists like Billy Graham and Oral Roberts have continued this tradition.

The late nineteenth century saw movements that aimed at an even more intense experience than did most revivals. The Holiness movement aimed at perfection in morality, simplicity in religion, and a deeper, heartfelt experience of God. The Pentecostal churches of the turn of the twentieth century went further: they sought a higher "blessing," usually the gift of speaking in tongues, a form of ecstatic speech attested in the New Testament. These different forms of a higher Christian life through inward experience continue to thrive today; Pentecostalism is popular not only among some sectarian Protestants but also in many Mexican-American Catholic churches, and the 1960s and 1970s saw it emerge among the white middle and upper classes, notably in the Roman Catholic and Episcopal denominations.

The inward turn of religious practice appeared in another, rather quiet, development of the nineteenth century: the growth of what we would today call meditative traditions. Often these combined the popular search for authentic experience with a more rational approach coming from the European Enlightenment and Romantic movements. In the United States, Transcendentalism, among the northeastern elites, was the intellectual side of that movement. Although the Transcendentalists are best known for their literary productions, their primary motivation came from a search for true inner experience, as in Ralph Waldo Emerson's "I become a transparent eyeball," or Henry David Thoreau's meditations on nature. Concurrently, at the popular level, the tradition of Spiritualism emerged in Europe and the United States. The Spiritualists were best known— and ridiculed—for their seances in which they tried to contact spirits of the dead as "scientific" proof that an afterlife existed, but they also shared a larger philosophy of which the seances were only a part. They held that the universe consisted of a harmonious unity of all things and that humans, by deepening their self-knowledge and their contact with other worlds, could live in greater harmony with God and with the All. This amorphous, loosely organized tradition began to achieve clearer definition in the latter part of the century, when New Thought and Christian Science (Mary Baker Eddy's Church of Christ, Scientist) appeared. Though these are in many respects independent movements—Mrs. Eddy insisted that hers had nothing to do with Spiritualism or other such popular traditions— they are clearly a part of the meditative tradition. Through specific practices of study and refocusing thought, Christian Scientists and New Thought practitioners attempt to bring the mind into harmony with the universal Mind, the power of healing in the universe, in order to gain power over material existence.

The growth of experiential Christianity went hand in hand with a voluntaristic emphasis: if each person's experience was valid, then each person could choose the appropriate church to suit his or her needs. This had dramatic effects on the churches. Where the eighteenth-century awakenings had produced temporary splits that healed (except for the Methodists), the nineteenth-century movements produced a rash of sectarianism, especially in the United States. Literally hundreds of new denominations began in the century between 1825 and 1925—some small and short-lived, others, like the Disciples of Christ, becoming major churches. In some cases the freedom to follow one's own experience also gave rise to prophets with new revelations. For example, in the early nineteenth century Joseph Smith claimed he had been visited by an angel who revealed to him the location of a great holy book. This book, translated under Smith's inspiration, became the Book of Mormon, foundation of the Church of Jesus Christ of Latter-day Saints (or Mormons). In the same era Ellen G. White, a member of a millennial sect, began receiving messages that led her, with others, to establish the doctrines and practices of the Seventh-day Adventists. Despite the emergence of some strong new churches, however, the concept of the church in general grew weaker. The church, for most American Protestants, was no longer an organic body, but a company of believers, each with his or her individual experiences that constituted the center of the religious life. The church therefore faced the danger of becoming merely another social gathering place.

The trends affected even the strongest church in the West, the Roman Catholic. During the nineteenth and early twentieth centuries, when European and immigrant communities remained strong in themselves, the Roman Catholic church kept a firm, though in the United States defensive, attachment to its traditions and doctrines.

By the mid-twentieth century, however, intellectual ferment and internal dissatisfaction had brought many people to question what seemed the anti-modern position of the church. In response, Pope John XXIII called the great Second Vatican Council (1962–65). The council adopted a declaration on religious freedom that urged tolerance of other religious ways and even other Christian churches; previously the church had regarded Protestants as heretics, outside the path of salvation. Major changes came in the liturgy: translation of the Mass into the language of each nation (previously it had been said wholly in Latin) and adaptations allowing greater time for congregational singing and for sermons. These changes reflected the Catholic church's support of the voluntary principle and a great willingness to allow for the importance of the worshiper's experience.

The experiential movement of the past two centuries has also led to an increase in missionary and reform activities. As often in a time of new religious movements, Christians with a strong inner sense of spiritual guidance become concerned about the condition of their society, or at least about the unsaved souls of their fellow human beings. On the whole, most such work has gone toward preaching the gospel to non-Christians at home or in foreign countries. Significant energy, however, has been directed toward political and social action: alleviating poverty, fighting disease and improving aid in underdeveloped countries, attending to the needs of the poor and elderly in the growing cities. Around the turn of the twentieth century some theologians, particularly in the United States, articulated a theological rationale for this emphasis, developing what they called the Social Gospel. In recent times theologians have developed "liberation" theologies that express a Christian commitment to the freedom and human rights of the oppressed people of the earth. Some of these outreach movements have been politically and socially conservative, others more radical. In general these movements have also allowed a larger religious role for women, though conservative churches have limited the definition of that role, and the role of pulpit minister is still largely dominated by men. Women have played a considerable part in the spread of experiential religion in general, as well as in spearheading many reforms.

Of course, the more emphasis among Christians on outreach and social action, the less energy is likely to be devoted to inner spiritual experience. For brief periods it has seemed that "social Christianity" has become the major force in modern development. Yet the repeated waves of revivals, awakenings, Pentecostal experiences, and devotional movements focusing on Jesus or on being "**born again**" show that the experiential movement that began some two centuries ago continues to be the major force in modern church movements. Social Christianity, apart from these movements, is the provenance of a small though important liberal wing. Theology is not dead, but it is largely confined to the seminaries; only in the Fundamentalist critique of modern culture do we find popular interest in theology and the doctrines of traditional Christianity. As for the sacramental life, some churches in recent times have expressed new interest in ritual; the Eastern Orthodox traditions have once again become important resources in that area. Such developments are minor, however, compared to the experiential movement and its offshoots, which, over a span of two hundred years, have brought about major changes in Christians' understanding of themselves, their churches, and their religious lives as a whole. In the next chapter, we will look at these developments in a different perspective, considering how they are related to the enduring structures of Christianity.

CHAPTER III

Structures of the Christian Life

L ike all religions Christianity can be understood through its structures as well as its history—that is, through its symbols, rituals, and institutions. The central structure in Christianity undoubtedly is its basic symbol: the figure of Jesus the Christ, represented graphically by the crucifix and the cross, symbols of his death and resurrection. The New Testament stories of Jesus have become common currency in Christian culture, but even apart from this, the various aspects of the religion cannot be understood without a grasp of the centrality of Jesus. The meanings of Christian rituals are based on stories about him, and the churches often regard their organizational forms as springing from his commands. The writings that describe Jesus' life and death, his acts and words, thus provide the founding myths of Christianity. These documents are structurally equivalent to the creation myths of other traditions, for they are the pivot around which the religion turns and to which it returns. This myth or set of myths is the fundamental story, containing the meaning of the religion. The different versions may or may not be true in the factual or historical sense; indeed, different Christian interpreters themselves disagree over the historical truth the myths contain. But they are "true" in that they are true to a particular vision of life; they are the seeds from which germinate the essential Christian practices and attitudes. The stories of Jesus encapsulate the spiritual truth of Christianity.

57

The Christian Story

The basic kernel of the stories is roughly as follows: Jesus was born in the reign of Herod the Great in Palestine, his birth being heralded by various signs of greatnerss even though his social status was humble (his father was a carpenter). His full appearance in the world came at the age of thirty, when he received baptism at the hands of John the Baptist. John was executed not long after, and Jesus began his own independent ministry. Different versions of the myth emphasize different aspects of his character, but in general they agree that he was a teacher and healer. As to his ultimate nature, some stories present him as a prophet (spokesman of God), others as the Messiah (God's chosen king), still others as God himself. He was expected to bring redemption not only to the Jewish people but to all peoples.

The versions that came to be included in the Christian New Testament give great prominence to Jesus' death. They tell that Jesus anticipated his own death and celebrated a "last supper" with his twelve disciples shortly before the Jewish Passover holiday.[4] One of the disciples, Judas, betrayed him, and Jesus was captured by the Romans, tried as a political rebel (for claiming to be the new Jewish king), and executed by being nailed to a cross. His body was taken down and buried, but after three days the body had disappeared. Some of his followers reported that angels had appeared, saying Jesus had risen from the dead; others then reported seeing him in several bodily appearances. This is the story of the Resurrection.

This basic myth has been the occasion for multiple interpretations throughout nearly two thousand years of Christian history. We cannot deal with them in depth, of course, but we must look at two important aspects of the way the story has been interpreted. On the one hand, Jesus has become a model for others to follow: the *imitatio Christi* (imitation of Christ) has become a guide for the Christian life. This is not unusual in religious traditions: the *imitatio Dei* (imitation of God) was and is a part of Judaism; Buddhists follow in the footsteps of the Buddha; and so on in many traditions. Later we will look at specific ways in which this has been true in Christianity. On the other hand, most Christian traditions have given special attention to the suffering, death, and resurrection of Jesus as a unique and miraculous event that brought about salvation for those who followed him. The story of Jesus is the story of salvation; it holds the keys to how to be saved. Salvation, then, is a central meaning of the myth. Here, the imitation of Christ becomes a participation in Christ, becoming a part of the great and mysterious events that, according to most Christians, transformed all of existence. We will first examine the concept of salvation, and then show how it has been elaborated in the life of the Christian community and of the individual believer.

The Meaning of Salvation

According to Christians, the fundamental divine miracle is the incarnation, death, and resurrection of Jesus; the church claims that this event had effects on the whole human race. Although different views of this miracle have appeared at different times in the history of Christian thought, most Christians would agree on a basic understanding of the event, briefly as follows: God became a human being in order to take on the state of sin, for sin constitutes the fundamental human condition since the fall of Adam and Eve, the first human beings according to the Bible. Yet although God-as-Jesus became human, he did not sin; nor (since he was God) did he have any stain of original sin inherited from Adam. Instead he suffered the punishment—namely, death—for the sin of the whole world. He was resurrected bodily from death, "redeemed" even from the world of the dead. From that time forward it would be possible for human beings also to be freed from the punishment for sin if they repented of sin, believed in Jesus as the Christ, and accepted the offer of salvation. "Repent and believe in the good news!" was the call of early Christian preachers. Beyond this, God offered to Christians and to the church as a body another gift, the Holy Spirit, as a continuing divine presence in their lives making them more like Christ himself.

The experience of salvation is accordingly a rebirth to a new life. The seeker moves from repentance and forgiveness, through the sacrifice of Christ, to taking on a new life in Christ and receiving the Holy Spirit. Since earliest times Christians have understood salvation in its original sense: it meant being saved, rescued, safe in a fortress besieged by the enemy. The related term *redemption* expresses a similar experience—being "bought back" from the evil powers by the gracious acts of God. The sense of evil afoot in the world and rooted deep in oneself is part of the basic Christian experience. With the experience of salvation, Christians feel freed from their anxiety, inner guilt, and sin and less subject to the demonic forces that seem to be bombarding them. That sense of freedom is the beginning; in addition, the experience of salvation brings a growing closeness to the divine and sometimes even ecstatic states, as if the Christian is being transported to higher levels of being. Salvation is thus a vividly real state of being connected to God, to the divine, that in a supportive Christian community may be an ongoing or a continually renewed experience.

Nevertheless, the state of present ecstasy sometimes diminishes in the churches. This should not surprise us. Often in new religious movements the early believers live in a high spiritual state of consciousness, with their positive experiences continually reinforced by the dedication of others around them. Later, however—especially in the second or third generation—the group's members may experience less of that ecstasy. Instead, if the group continues, they look to the future and emphasize the experience of hope. This happens in Christianity as well. One generation of Christians may have an immediate sense of the divine presence in their lives, whereas later ones, who no longer find that experience available to them, focus on future hopes. Such hopes come quite naturally to Christianity, which grew up among Jewish groups alive with the expectation of a messiah and in a Greek environment filled with hopes of personal immortality after death. In this context, salvation has also come to refer to the state Christians would experience after death. As early as the writings of Paul, we can see a tension between the present state of salvation and the even greater life that is promised when the Messiah returns: now Christians are "justified," Paul writes—that is, they are put in a right relation to God—later they will be "sanctified," made perfectly holy. Christianity fluctuates between the two poles, sometimes becoming very otherworldly, at other times emphasizing the quest for spiritual experience in the present.

It is important to recognize that, whether salvation is conceived in terms of present experience or of future promise, the reality of salvation has almost always been mediated through ritual. In some varieties of Christianity the primary rituals have been the receiving of the sacraments; in others, the discipline of a life of prayer and contemplation has led toward the higher life. Preaching, singing, or personal interaction have been channels through which a person might experience salvation from sin or the blessings of the Holy Spirit. Salvation can be a highly personal, transcendent experience, an encounter of the individual Christian with the divine. But on the earthly plane it is expressed as an initiation, a ritual leading to new birth. The early church developed a series of rituals as vehicles of that transforming experience: a period of study and testing; the rites of baptism and confirmation; and the first partaking of the Eucharist.

Spiritual Knowledge: Creed and Doctrine in Christianity

As in most initiations, the candidate has to pass a test, and the testing in Christianity has revolved around knowledge of spiritual things, particularly the creed. People wishing to enter a Christian church, of course, had to be of good moral character, and the priest or bishop would watch them closely for their sincerity and willingness to lead upright lives. Their study was central, however; in the early church they spent nearly a year learning the beliefs and rites of the church, particularly the meaning of the incarnation, death, and resurrection of Jesus. Before baptism the candidate would be asked questions, probably a triple question for the triple immersion. We do not have the exact text of any such examination, but it probably went something like the following: "Do you believe in God the Father, maker of heaven and earth? Do you believe in Jesus the Son, who suffered, died, and rose again? Do you believe in the Holy Spirit in the Holy Church?" The questioning was, of course, a formality; someone who had gone through the course of study was unlikely to answer no. Nevertheless, the examination symbolized an important aspect of Christian existence; belief in the appropriate creed was a crucial standard for belonging to the community.

Yet against the background of other religions this is quite remarkable: no other major tradition puts so great an emphasis on belief, on correct thinking, on affirming the correct words. Most traditions emphasize practice far more than belief. Why did Christianity take this path? An important reason is that the culture in which Christianity came to flower, the Hellenistic culture of the Mediterranean, valued philosophy and, indeed, linked religion closely to philosophy. Philosophy itself had a religious aura—the philosopher was a lover of Wisdom, who often was portrayed as a semi-divine, usually feminine, being (Sophia in Greek, Chokmah in Hebrew). The great Roman orator Cicero regarded the faculty of reason as being the mode by which the soul could ascend to the divine. Hellenistic philosophies usually viewed the soul as essentially rational and held that God expressed himself through Mind.

Thus Christianity, as it began its work of theology, of systematically elucidating the nature of God and his revelation to human beings, referred to similar concepts. When the Gospel of John declared, "In the beginning was the Word [*Logos*]," the author was asserting that Jesus was to be understood as a revelation of the divine Mind. As we saw in Chapter II, Logos theology was prominent among the early apologists. Christians thus set out the path to God in terms of a path to wisdom, explicit in stating and reasoning out the things one had to know. Clarity of thought in matters of religion meant freedom of movement, a clear path to God. Incorrect understanding could lead to one's worshiping the wrong God, following the wrong savior or leader. Part of the responsibility that the church took on, one of the ways it became a vehicle of salvation, was to smooth the path by establishing right belief and right understanding.

This task came to a focus in the creeds of the churches. Creeds (from the Latin *credere*, to believe) are simply statements of belief. From very early, however, they became part of public worship: part of paying homage to God was stating one's belief. This practice had precedent in Judaism, where the Shema (a statement of the Jewish covenant with God, beginning "Hear O Israel, the Lord is our God, the Lord is One") and its accompanying blessings contain some affirmations of faith. But the theological-philosophical emphasis of Hellenistic culture made the creeds of the daughter religion somewhat different. We can see the careful statement of issues by looking at samples of early creeds. The first example here is the Roman creed as known from fourth-century texts; the second, the so-called Apostles' Creed, was generally used in the West from about the sixth century and is still used in many Protestant churches today. The third, the Nicene Creed, is in general use, with slight variations, in Eastern Orthodox and, since the Council of Trent, in Roman Catholic churches. The form given here is the current one, very close to the Constantinople formula of 381.

Roman:

I believe in God the Father Almighty,

And in Jesus Christ, his only Son, our Lord,

Who was born by the Holy Ghost, of the Virgin Mary, was crucified under Pontius Pilate, and was buried.

The third day he rose from the dead,

He ascended into heaven and sits on the right hand of the Father;

From thence he will come to judge the quick and the dead.

And in the Holy Ghost, the Holy Church, the forgiveness of sins, the resurrection of the body.

Apostles' Creed:

I believe in God the Father Almighty, Maker of heaven and earth, and in Jesus Christ, his only Son, our Lord, who was conceived by the Holy Ghost, born of the Virgin Mary, suffered under Pontius Pilate, was crucified, dead, and buried. He descended into Hell.

The third day he rose from the dead, he ascended into heaven and sits on the right hand of God the Father Almighty.

From thence he will come to judge the quick and the dead.

I believe in the Holy Ghost, the Holy Catholic Church, the communion of saints, the forgiveness of sins, the resurrection of the body, and the life everlasting.

Nicene Creed:

We believe in one God the Father Almighty, Maker of heaven and earth, and of all things visible and invisible.

And in one Lord Jesus Christ, the only begotten Son of God, begotten of the Father before all worlds,

Light of Light, Very God of Very God,

Begotten, not made, being of one substance with the Father, by whom all things were made,

Who for us men, and for our salvation, came down from heaven,

And was incarnate by the Holy Ghost of the Virgin Mary, and was
    made man.
He was crucified for us under Pontius Pilate, and suffered and was
    buried.
And the third day he rose again, according to the Scriptures, and
    ascended into heaven, and sits on the right hand of the Father,
And he shall come again, with glory, to judge the quick and the
    dead; Whose kingdom shall have no end.
And in the Holy Ghost, the Lord, and Giver of life;
Who proceeds from the Father, Who with the Father and the Son
    together is worshipped and glorified,
Who spoke by the Prophets.
And in one holy catholic and apostolic Church.
We acknowledge one baptism for the remission of sins, and we look
    for the resurrection of the dead, and the life of the world to
    come.

In these creeds we can trace the evidences of numerous theological debates. The Roman creed did not need to specify that God was "maker of heaven and earth," but both other creeds did, countering Gnostic asertions that the true God could not have created the evil material world. The Nicene emphasis that he made "all things visible and invisible" reflects the church's conflict with Manichaeanism beginning in the late third century: the prophet Mani taught that the world was a battleground between good and evil and, like the Gnostics, that there was an evil god who had created the visible world and invisible demonic forces. The Apostles' and Nicene creeds also emphasize the suffering of Jesus over against the Docetists, who claimed that Jesus' human form was not real. The fourth-century debate with Arius over the relation of Jesus' humanity to his divinity lies behind the careful statements of the Nicene: Jesus was begotten, not made (Arius claimed Jesus was a created being), and was of the same substance as God the Father (some theologians argued he was only of similar substance). One could go on; virtually every phrase is the result of untold hours of thought, argument, and reflection.

The creeds gave rise to dogma (literally, "teaching"), for the faithful needed to have fuller instruction as to what the church affirmed and why. Not all branches of Christianity have given the same significance to doctrine and theological understanding, however. For the Orthodox churches, dogma was essential, but truth was fully confirmed only by one's experience in the worshiping community. In the early Middle Ages in the West, any education was a rarity; few learned even to read, let alone argue theology. From the eleventh century onward, however, theology emerged into prominence again. In the High Middle Ages theology was regarded as "queen of the sciences," the capstone of knowledge, which unified all the partial truths of the various branches of learning. The Protestant Reformers used theology as one of their primary weapons against Roman Catholicism, arguing that many Catholic errors stemmed from theological misunderstandings. Therefore the Protestant churches reformulated many basic dogmas of the church and wrote lengthy catechisms like the Westminster Confession (Calvinist). For several centuries the rival Protestant sects thrived on theological argument among themselves. Even the nineteenth-century American frontier churches held spirited theological debates, although the people were poorly educated. The Protestant emphasis on Scripture gave people a concrete foundation for argument, so that even relatively unlearned persons could "theologize," so to speak, on the basis of specific passages in the New Testament. On the other hand, despite the high level of education in the twentieth century, theology has declined in importance again.

Yet, on the whole, creed and doctrine have been very important defining characteristics of a Christian; they are not merely traditional formulas but expressions of a deep acceptance of the faith. The implicit assumption is that the most profound acceptance requires the concurrence of the great human faculty of intellect: the mind itself must grasp the ideas of the faith if the person is to be truly bound to them. Indeed, the highest levels of mind are engaged—those levels that approach the divine. Once the mind is trained to spiritual things, then the individual can approach the great mysteries: the rites of the church.

The Drama of Transformation: From Baptism to Eucharist

Baptism is clearly the primary Christian rite of initiation. Sometimes it is highly dramatic; at other times it appears largely perfunc-

tory. But in any case it is understood as a powerful re-enactment of
the death (through immersion) and resurrection (coming out of the
water) of Jesus himself. Of course, baptism also imitates Jesus' baptism by John in the Jordan River. Further, Judaism already had a
similar ritual of conversion: a long period of study and examination
followed by immersion in a naturally constituted body of water;
there, as in many other religions, immersion symbolized the death of
the old person and rebirth of the new. For Christians it was appropriate to adapt this ritual to their new understanding of existence: as
Jesus had died and been "reborn," so with every Christian. Thus
Paul wrote in his letter to the church at Rome:

> Do you not know that all of us who have been baptized into Christ
> Jesus were baptized into his death? We were buried therefore with
> him by baptism into death, so that as Christ was raised from the dead
> by the glory of the Father, so we too might walk in newness of life.
> (Rom. 6:3–4, RSV)

The drama of baptism, which in the early church was usually on
Easter morning after a fast and an all-night vigil, culminated with
the new Christian donning white garments, a symbol of purity and
new birth that is echoed in the white baptismal gowns of babies
even today.

*The dramatic event of
baptism in the early
church often took place in
a specially designed bap-
tismal font. This, the
Baptistry of St. John La-
teran in Rome, was ori-
ginally built in the time of
Constantine, and rebuilt
by later popes. Photo used
by permission of Hirmer
Archive, Munich.*

The next part of the initiation is confirmation—originally an anointing with consecrated oil, the "Christing" of the believer—for *Christos* meant "anointed one"—like a king. In this act the believer becomes like Christ and at this moment receives the gift of the Holy Spirit. Just as the Spirit descended on Jesus in the shape of a dove after he came up out of the Jordan, so the oil of anointing represents the descent of the Spirit on the Christian. The rite of confirmation is still practiced immediately after baptism in Eastern Orthodox churches; Roman Catholics and most Protestants perform it at a time when the person has reached an age of understanding. In churches where ecstatic experience is the goal, for example the Pentecostal, the gift of the Holy Spirit has again come into prominence as the mark of the true Christian, although it is not usually considered a ritual of confirmation.

After baptism and (usually) confirmation, the convert comes for the first time to the Eucharist, literally the "thanksgiving" service, the meal celebrated on Sunday mornings in honor of the Lord's Day by full members of the church. In the early church, candidates were excluded from this part entirely, even as observers; they could attend services only to the point where selections from the Bible were read and a sermon was preached. Their first Communion after baptism therefore would have been a special event: at last they were part of the inner circle, the intimate community of the church. In the early decades this was indeed a small group, a dedicated band meeting quietly to avoid detection in times of persecution. Their meals, at which they ritually remembered Jesus and re-enacted his last meeting with his disciples, would have been charged with tension, excitement, and joyous fellowship. Yet the meaning of the Eucharist did not depend on the feelings of the believers present; even when baptism and confirmation became less dramatic, the Eucharist remained powerful and mysterious. It continued as the heart of Christian worship for centuries.

We can develop some sense of the meaning of the Eucharist by looking at the way it was most likely practiced in the churches of the first hundred years of Christianity.[5] The rite began with a greeting from the bishop to the people: "Peace be with you." They responded, "And with your spirit." The congregation exchanged the kiss of peace, men to men and women to women. The laypeople brought

their offerings, a small loaf of bread and a little wine in a flask. The
deacons received them and laid them on the altar, pouring the wines
into larger flasks. The bishop and the presbyters ("elders," primarily
church administrators) rinsed their hands and then laid hands on the
offerings. The bishop recited the eucharistic prayer of thanks to
God. The deacons or bishop broke the loaves, they partook, and
then the bishop himself distributed it to the people, saying, "The
Bread of heaven." Presbyters and deacons then distributed the wine,
and also water, to the people, who came up in a row to receive three
sips from each cup. At each sip the one who held the cup said, "In
God the Father Almighty," "And in the Lord Jesus Christ," and
then "And in the Holy Spirit in the Holy Church," with the recipient responding, "Amen." After this the vessels were washed and the
communicants dismissed.

The ritual had three prominent dimensions, each of them important to the new Christian. The Eucharist was a joyous communal
feast; it was a sacrifice; and it communicated great spiritual power.
The communal nature would have been evident from the beginning, with the exchange of greetings and the kiss of peace; here was
the good will and intimacy of a group of people who felt almost like
a family. Moreover, each person had his or her role in an organic and
interdependent society: the layperson brought an offering, the deacon presented and distributed the offerings; the bishop consecrated
the ordinary bread and wine to be spiritual food. The community
ate together, solemnly, affirming their unity, becoming more truly
one in Christ. The Eastern church called the Eucharist a wedding
feast, celebrating the union of Christ with his bride, the church. And
as at a wedding, the community overcomes its differences and becomes one in rejoicing with bride and groom.

Second, the Eucharist was a sacrifice: each member brought
something, a gift of his or her own substance in the form of bread or
wine, to become part of the sacrifice. The form is reminiscent of the
practice of sacrifice in many societies: the person who has sinned or
who desires a spiritual benefit brings an animal or some loaves or
fruit as offerings to the divine source of life. In giving over part of
oneself, one participates in a vital exchange with the deity. In Christianity, this fundamental structure is amplified: the offering one
brings becomes transformed into the body of Christ, who is God,
who has sacrificed himself for the benefit of all. The food offered

becomes divine through the cosmic miracle of Jesus' suffering and death; one eats not bread and wine but the body and blood of Christ.

In this miracle, the sacrifice releases great spiritual power, an infusion of spiritual nourishment for the Christian. For this reason some Christians have wished to partake of it often. The development of the "low mass," which requires only one other person to be present besides the priest, came from the wish of priests to commune daily for their spiritual nourishment. At the same time, the extreme holiness of the rite, the sense that it held enormous power, kept some away: about the fifth century the laity stopped communing each Sunday because they felt too impure to approach the altar; it also became the practice that only the priests would drink the wine, and the laypeople would take only the bread. Nevertheless, the meal remained the "bread of heaven" and the body of Christ. As Theodotus of Egypt (ca. 160) wrote, "The bread is hallowed by the power of the name of God. . . . It is transformed into spiritual power."

Because of the enormous power associated with the Eucharist, the awesomeness of the idea of God's sacrifice, and the sense of unity it generated in the church, Christians throughout the ages have entered into the ritual with humility, awe, and gratitude. The taking of holy food has been the spiritual nourishment of the church continually, week to week, in the celebration of the Lord's Day. As the culmination of the initiation of a new believer, the Eucharist has been a most powerful ritual: the seeker of salvation becomes a part of a holy community.

The Church as Holy Community

From the beginning the churches conceived of themselves as a corporate entity; Paul called it "the body of Christ":

> For just as the body is one and has many members, and all the members of the body, though many, are one body, so it is with Christ. For by one Spirit we were all baptized into one body—Jews or Greeks, slaves or free—and all were made to drink of one Spirit. . . . Now you are the body of Christ and individually members of it. And God has appointed in the church first apostles, second prophets, third teachers,

then workers of miracles, then healers, helpers, administrators, speakers in various kinds of tongues. (1 Cor. 12–13, 27–28, RSV)

The many roles mentioned by Paul devolved into three "orders," as we have seen—the laity, the deacons, and the bishops—with the presbyters, or elders, being the administrators. As more priests were needed, the priesthood became the order of which the bishop was the authoritative head (archbishops and cardinals appeared still later as the church needed a clear hierarchy of organization). The three primary orders each had their own role to play, interdependently, but the community fully affirmed its unity in the rites of the Eucharist. The bishops, further, understood themselves as continuing the intimate community of Jesus and his disciples; the pope regarded himself as the successor of Peter, who headed the disciples after Jesus' death. Moreover, a great spiritual event in the life of the church happened communally. Tradition as recorded in the Book of Acts tells that fifty days after the Resurrection, probably on the Jewish holiday of Shavuot (Greek, Pentecost), the followers who gathered in Jerusalem experienced a gift of the Holy Spirit, including ecstatic behavior like speaking in tongues. They received a spiritual experience of unity; they were as one person at Pentecost. Like the Jews who together had seen the splitting of the Red Sea as they left Egypt, and together had heard God's voice while standing at Sinai to receive the Ten Commandments, Christians now claimed to experience God's revelation not just to individuals but to the group as a whole. Similarly, the church fathers held that the church partakes of the Eucharist corporately, not as individuals. The community is one being.

This strong sense of community appears in the repeated attempts of various groups to purify the church. In the fourth century a major movement led by Donatus attempted to purify the church in Africa. He and his followers believed that no bishop who had given in to Diocletian's persecution (284–305) by handing over holy Scriptures or other church property should be allowed to hold office. The mainstream church, led by Augustine, concluded that the church on earth could not be expected to be so pure. As Augustine put it, the "invisible church," comprising the **elect** whom only God could know, would remain pure; the "visible church" here on earth would always include some sinners. Nevertheless, the presence of sinners—even among those who performed the sacraments—would not divert the church from its true course, or prevent the elect from gaining their salvation. Yet, despite the defeat of the Donatists, movements of purification appeared repeatedly. The Cathars of the Middle Ages and the Puritans of England and America are only two major examples of groups who believed they alone constituted the true or pure church. The ultimate recourse of such movements appears in the life of Roger Williams, founder of Rhode Island colony. He separated from the main body of Puritans to found his own Baptist church; then, finding its members were too impure, he eventually separated from them and would worship in company with no one but his wife—and sometimes not her.

Such movements illustrate a central conviction of Christians through the ages: the worshipers called the church are tied together in an intimate way. If they are one body, then the leg affects what the arm does, and both influence the liver and kidneys. The members of a Christian church are not independent; what each does affects the others. Moreover, the church should be as much like Christ as possible. Thus some Christians have believed that the presence of sinners would bring disastrous results on all, so they undertook to purify the church, making it more truly the body of Christ. A similar impulse arises among Christian groups who seek to minimize their contact with the world. By forming nearly self-sufficient communities, like the villages of the Amish in Pennsylvania or Ohio, they can try to keep their group untainted. By adopting specific rules limiting interaction with others, as when some churches forbid marriage to nonmembers or some born-again Christian movements encourage buying goods only from other born-again Christians, they increase their consciousness of the holiness and purity of their own community.

The deep sense of interrelatedness in the church, the conviction that all are truly one body, can help us understand how priests or monks have sometimes functioned on behalf of the whole church. The various orders of the early church worked like different groups of organs within a body; as people pursued their spiritual quest more intensely, however, other "orders" emerged. The early church had an order of penitents (as we will see); later, the orders of monks, nuns, and friars emerged; and even pilgrims became a kind of unofficial "order" in the Middle Ages. Some of these people seemed especially holy because of their religious dedication, and the church at large came to regard them as a stream of spiritual power from which the whole body could drink. Those who were unable to or who preferred not to take on such religious tasks performed the more material work of sustaining the church. Thus from a group where all were "saints," as the early church called members, the church developed into an organization in which certain groups became higher-level specialists in the spiritual realm. The few who dedicated themselves wholly to God became the more spiritual organs, and as such came to represent the Holy Church itself. Thus at certain times the church regarded the monks' prayers as communicating with God on behalf of the whole church, and the priest could perform the Eucharist, the communal event par excellence, with as few as one other person communing with him.

Each of these specialized roles was an imitation of Christ as well as being representative of the whole body. The bishop, for example, was leader of his flock in the same way that Jesus had led his band of disciples. According to an early tradition, Jesus handed the mantle of leadership to Peter (the name means "rock"), saying, "On this rock I will build my church." This became an authoritative statement for one particular leadership pattern. The flock would have one shepherd, like Jesus and then Peter, as head of the apostles after Jesus' death. The bishop therefore was to take Jesus' place: he usually celebrated the Eucharist, distributing bread and wine to the people just as Jesus did at the Last Supper. He was also the teacher, as Jesus had taught. For example, in the fourth century, Jesus was portrayed on sarcophagi as teaching a group of men from a book—a teacher of wisdom like the philosophers of the day. During that same period congregations expected their bishops to deliver learned lectures on Sundays, expounding the true wisdom as revealed in Christ. As a group, the bishops together became like another band of disciples who guided the church as a whole.

Secular leaders could take on the model of Christ as well. Eastern emperors regarded themselves as bearing the mantle of a Christly king and almost a priest, and when monarchy became the form of government in medieval Europe, the kings saw themselves as imitating the heavenly kingship of the resurrected Christ. The crowning of a monarch included the religious ceremony of anointing with oil. The king performed what were considered religious functions and had supernatural powers: like Christ who would return to judge all,

The emperor as the representative of Christ on earth is illustrated by the cross in the left hand and the scepter of rulership in the right. Here the Emperor Otto II is depicted on the Master of the Registrum Gregorii, a book made in Trier, France, about 983. Used by permission of Editions d'Art Albert Skira, Geneva.

the king was judge; like Christ who sacrificed himself on behalf of humans, the king interceded between the people and God to protect them. Kings occupied a special place between the heavenly and earthly realms, like Jesus who was both human and divine. Some people even believed that kings could heal the sick and make crops grow. In short, the king was a religious personality like a bishop. One chronicler, Bishop Otto of Freising, wrote after observing the coronation of a German king that

> On the same day and in the same church, the elected bishop of Munster was consecrated by the same prelates who had anointed the king. . . . as a favorable presage for the future, since the same church and the same day witnessed the unction of the two persons who . . . are the only persons sacramentally anointed, each alike entitled *Christus Domini.*[6]

All kinds of leaders thus took on holiness by making themselves like Christ.

Outside the regular leadership roles other manifestations of holiness revealed the *imitatio Christi*. For example, the martyrs of the early centuries took on the mantle of Christ; it was a great calling in times of persecution to die for Christ. This was not entirely new—Jews reckoned it an honor to die *al kiddush Hashem*, while sanctifying the name of God. Christians gave the martyr's death an additional value, however, because Jesus had died a violent death at the hands of persecutors. To die in that way meant coming near to Christ, participating in his sacrifice, and partaking of his glory. The bishop of Antioch near the end of the first century C.E., Ignatius, looked forward with an almost sensuous delight to following in the footsteps of Jesus by becoming a martyr. He pleaded with his friends not to intervene in his behalf:

> Grant me nothing more than that I should be poured out as a libation to God, while there is still an altar ready. . . . I am God's wheat, and I am ground by the teeth of wild beasts, that I may be found pure bread. . . . Entreat Christ for me, that through these beasts I may be found a sacrifice to God.[7]

Ignatius got his wish: he died at the hands of the Romans, who threw him to the lions in 110 C.E.

The model of Christ has become an important motif in the ascetic movements of Christianity as well. Those who wanted to follow Jesus when there was no more outside persecution could engage in their own battles with the demonic forces that ruled the world. As Jesus had battled demons in his contest with Satan, the monks of the desert or the cloister could fight the evil forces within themselves. By conquering the temptations of the world, by giving up its luxuries and pleasures and instead devoting oneself to prayer and praise of God, one could be following Jesus' command, "Be ye perfect." Saint Francis of Assisi in the thirteenth century offered another version of the model, vowing to be an itinerant, never having a roof over his head and never owning anything. Popular asceticism included even more dramatic examples, like the flagellants of the late Middle Ages who marched in procession, beating themselves with whips or thorns to symbolize their identification with the sufferings of Jesus. Thus monks, martyrs, bishops, and kings all represented an intensification of the imitation of Christ within the structure of the church, whether by asceticism, sacrifice, or the taking on of spiritual leadership. As religious specialists, they have helped to ensure the holiness of the community as a whole.

At various times some groups of Christians have criticized that sort of specialization, insisting instead that the church as a whole is holy, and no one in the church is any more holy than anyone else. The Protestant Reformation, as we saw in Chapter II, virtually erased the older structure of orders on behalf of the idea of the "priesthood of all believers": any member could perform the specialized spiritual function, for example, of receiving another member's confession. Many small evangelical sects follow the principle that there should not be any ordained minister or preacher, that anyone who feels the call to preach may do so. The Quaker meeting is another version of that principle: all sit quietly until a person's "inner light" leads him or her to speak or pray. Nevertheless, the idea of spiritual specialization did not entirely die. The larger Protestant tradition maintained the requirement that those who would interpret Scripture—the clergy—must have specialized training. They are not inherently more holy, but their education represents their devotion and dedication, just as other special practices did for the monks. Even the idea that one should have a spiritual "calling" to preach (whether that calling is temporary or for a lifetime) suggests again the idea of spiritual specialization. In the popular mind missionaries and other dedicated Christian teachers have earned some of the status given to religious orders; they are regarded as possessing special grace that enables them to endure unusual hardships and trials. And even in Protestantism the reluctance of churches to pay their ministers high salaries indicates not the stinginess of congregations but the persistent sense that the Christian leader should be less tempted by worldly things, by the things that money can buy. Thus, on the one hand, there have been repeated movements for democratization of the church, emphasizing that all are equally holy; on the other, the holy community has always had leaders who, officially or unofficially, are the spiritual specialists—those who possess a special dedication or spiritual intensity that benefits the church as a whole.

The Life of the Church

Drawn together as a holy community, energized by its dedicated spiritual leaders, the church lives as a corporate being, an organic entity moving through time. It partakes of the Holy Spirit as regular nourishment, through the Eucharist or Holy Communion in most churches (though some celebrate it infrequently), and also through the preached Word in the Protestant churches. Moreover, the church is the vehicle of the Holy Spirit in the world, the embodiment of the third person of the Trinity as Jesus embodied the second person. The church therefore aims to continue the work of Christ on earth: to bring salvation to humanity, to unite humanity with divinity. We can see this work as having three parts, each modeled on a different aspect of the life of Christ: evangelism, calling people outside the church to repent and believe; the work of salvation proper, enacted in the regular liturgies of the church; and the work of establishing the messianic kingdom under the rule of Christ. In each of these, the church as a body imitates Christ.

As the story of Jesus tells that he went about preaching the coming of God's kingdom, inviting people to enter, so the church has as one of its primary tasks the spreading of the gospel or "good news" to all people. Though Jesus preached to Jews, the church from early times has interpreted its mission far more widely: the apostles were to preach to all nations, to the ends of the earth. Among the various churches the message at its core has been nearly universal: all have sinned, but God has provided a remedy for sin in the work of Jesus the Christ; turn from sin and believe in Christ and you will receive the gift of salvation and eternal life. Usually the church has appointed special teachers or missionaries for the work of going out to the non-Christian world. Yet every believer also bears some responsibility for witnessing, that is, attesting to the truth of the Christian message in the presence of those who are not part of the church.

The evangelistic work, however, is only the beginning. As we have seen, the rites of baptism, confirmation, and the first Communion introduce the convert into the community. But rituals are also essential to maintain the community and continue the work of salvation. The church as a body has, from early times, held that it was nourished by the regular weekly sharing of the Eucharist. For the Eastern church, as mentioned earlier, this rite embodies the union of humanity with divinity and is appropriately called the Divine Liturgy. In the setting of the church, the icons mirror the heavenly presence of Jesus, Mary, saints and angels. The Eucharist itself is a wedding feast, uniting Christ with his church, his two "bodies" as it were, and presaging the great re-union which will take place when Christ returns at the end of time. As this holy union is repeated week after week, the church and its members, sharing in the feast, are continually reconnected with their divine source of life.

The metaphor that in the West dominates the Eucharist is that of sacrifice. According to Roman Catholic theology, each repetition of the rite actually re-enacts the original sacrifice of Jesus (though not his physical death). In an awesome event, Jesus gives himself entirely to God and God in Jesus gives himself to save human beings from eternal death. The sacrifice reflects an archaic structure: a part of the whole (for example one's crops or herds) is given to ensure continuing fruitfulness. Here, one death is given in order that all humanity may receive fullness of life. Partaking of the body and blood of the one sacrificed is the source of continuing spiritual nourishment of the Western church.

Protestant churches have de-emphasized the Eucharist, many churches treating it only as a memorial rather than as a present and immediate spiritual event. Instead, they have turned to the preached word as the source of spiritual nourishment. The sermon based on Scripture offers a different kind of ritual experience for the church. Rather than the taking of food, which involves taste and texture combined with the visual drama of the priest's actions, the altar, the statues or icons, we find a focus on hearing and mental action, taking in with the ear and assimilating with the mind. The spiritual transformation takes place not through the tactile and visual senses, but from the top downward, so to speak, through ear and mind to the rest of the person.

Here, too, there are significant variations within the Protestant tradition. Some churches emphasize the learned discourse; others, the immediacy of spiritual calling that leads a person to preach spontaneously. The first emphasizes the rational mind: Scripture is given to the church as its source of spiritual guidance, and to grasp it Christians must use their minds. They must study, reflect, and think through carefully to unravel the mysteries of the holy Word. The second focuses on inspiration or intuition: since Scripture is a mystery, only those possessed by the Spirit can understand it; study is less relevant. The one appeals to the rational mind and aims at a sense of satisfaction through convincing argument; the other appeals to the aesthetic and intuitive and aims at an experience of unity through congruence of scriptural passages with everyday experience. Most Protestant churches, of course, expect a mixture of the two: a learned lecturer without spirit or aesthetic quality sounds dead; high spirit without some thought about the content and some familiarity with the Bible is, as the saying goes, nothing but hot air. The two bring together both poles of the Protestant worship experience to a synthesis of the mind, which then inspires the whole person and the whole church.

That is the regular course of ritual; but the life of the church involves more than the weekly partaking of the Spirit through word and sacrament. The church moves through time, repeating the work of Jesus himself by re-creating each year the cycle of the major events of his life and celebrating them in the round of the calendar. From the birth of Jesus and the visit of the wise men to the Resurrection and the descent of the Holy Spirit on the church, the yearly cycle recognizes the special times in Jesus' life. The church as the body of Christ acknowledges them and, by participating in them, experiences their holiness. In addition the Catholic and Orthodox churches celebrate feast days of saints—those who by virtue of their holy lives are closest to the model of Jesus himself. The saints' days are feasts of the church celebrating the Holy Spirit at work in its own community, within the body as it now lives, making the yearly round more nearly divine with the experiences of its own members.

The major seasons of the Christian year begin with Advent (literally "the coming"), which looks forward to the birth of Jesus. Although the date of Christmas was not established until the fourth century (and Catholic and Orthodox still disagree), once a date was established it became a major festival with its own seasonal rites. From the Sunday nearest Saint Andrew's feast (November 30), that is, approximately four weeks before Christmas on December 25, special prayers and hymns appear in church services, and the priest or minister offers sermons appropriate for the occasion. The Western Christmas season itself does not end with the Nativity but goes on for twelve days more, culminating in the Epiphany on January 6, when according to tradition the three wise men from the East arrived to pay homage to the infant Jesus. For the church this represented the first manifestation of the Christ to the world at large. (January 6 is also the day established in Orthodox churches for Christmas.) For the church the entire season is one of joy and hope, full of the expectation of Jesus and the transformation he will bring. Like the birth of a child in a family, the Nativity brings excitement and happy fellowship as the church unites around the re-enactment of the appearance of Jesus in the world. Nativity plays, popular among children and adults through the centuries, are a simple but profound expression of that special sort of joy. The season is also, of course, that of the winter solstice, a time when many traditions express their hope and expectation of the renewal of the world as the days grow gradually longer and greater light returns to the earth. Christmas sanctifies that hope in a Christian light, and undoubtedly the presence of pagan celebrations at that time contributed to the final establishment of a winter date for Jesus' birth.

The next major season begins in late winter with the onset of Lent, forty days before Easter. This was originally the time for the final preparation of the candidates for baptism, with prescribed fasting and serious repentance, a final turning away from sin. When the sacrament of penance developed, the penitents often had to serve their special duties for the length of Lent. Gradually the whole church joined the **catechumens** and penitents in making Lent a period of self-examination, repentance, and abstinence (for example, abstinence from rich foods like meat). Thus the period became a somber and reflective one, looking forward toward the coming suffering of Christ.

The day before Lent begins, Shrove Tuesday, became in many countries a carnival day. First it was celebrated in Italy, then it spread to France and Spain; the French brought it to New Orleans as Mardi Gras ("Fat Tuesday"). In England, it was called Pancake Day, the day on which one should use up all one's fats and oils, which were considered rich and luxurious foods. The wild carnival atmosphere gives way to Ash Wednesday, so named because many would attend Mass and have ashes smeared on their foreheads as a sign of penitence. Lent culminates in the services of Holy Week, the last week before Easter. Palm Sunday, the Sunday before Easter, reminds the church of Jesus' triumphal entry into Jerusalem, and is a day of high spirit anticipating Easter. Afterward, however, the church becomes solemn again with Maundy Thursday, the day of the Last Supper of Jesus with his disciples, so called because at this time, tradition says, Jesus gave two commands (mandates, from which "Maundy" is derived): "Do this in remembrance of me" and "Love one another as I have loved you." The church remembers also the betrayal of Judas and Jesus' agony in the garden of Gethsemane as he faced his death. The next day, Good Friday, recalls his trial and crucifixion. Deep sadness penetrates the church, and altars and pulpits are often draped in black.

Easter, preceded in the early church by an all-night vigil on Saturday night, brings a total change of mood to joy and rebirth from the depths of despair. Even today, though the vigil is a rarity, sunrise services celebrate the renewal of life symbolized by the resurrection of Jesus from the tomb. One of the great festivals of the early church, Easter celebrates purity as well as joy; this was the time when new members were baptized, coming forth from the water to don their white robes. Easter is dated on the first Sunday after the first full moon following the spring equinox, and it coincides in northern latitudes with the beginning of spring, echoing at another level the gift of newness of life.

Forty days later, on a Thursday, is the traditional date of Jesus' ascension into heaven, a major feast in Catholicism and Orthodoxy. It anticipates the great festival of the "fiftieth day," Pentecost (always on a Sunday, for Easter is counted as day one). Here the church celebrates the gift of the Holy Spirit. This is also, of course, a festive holiday, but more than the joy of newness Pentecost relives the endowment of spiritual power given to the church, the sense of transformation to another level of existence. It also looks toward taking up the work of the church, which is the successor to Jesus himself: announcing the good news to others and establishing God's kingdom on earth. One week later Trinity Sunday celebrates the oneness of God's three revelations as Father, Son, and Holy Spirit.

The importance of the round of the Christian year is accented in many churches by the use of special vestments and tapestries for each season. The pattern of Christ's life as model for the church is, in addition, repeated over and over again in Christian art. The architectural form of the church itself became, in the Middle Ages, an expression both of the spiritual reality of the church as image of Christ and of the heavenly world to which Christians looked forward. The floor plan followed the shape of the cross: being in the church implied being with the "body" of Christ crucified and resurrected. The church's altar stood at the eastern wall, facing Jerusalem where the crucifixion had occurred; the western portal, the main en-

The millennium, or ex-
pected thousand-year reign
of Christ, has at times been
a major topic of Christian
study and speculation.
This illustration was the
front cover of a medieval
commentary on the book of
Revelation. Beatus of Lie-
bana's Commentaries on
the Apocalypse: The
Coming of the End of the
World *(France, mid-elev-
enth century). An angel
trumpets and a third of the
sun and moon are dark-
ened, while an eagle cries,
"Woe, woe, woe...!"
(Rev. 8:13). Photo used by
permission of Bibliothèque
Nationale, Paris.*

trance, was often decorated with a dramatic scene of Judgment Day
or of Christ in triumph, suggesting the future destiny of the church.
Scenes from the life of Christ have been painted, woven into tapestries, or portrayed in stained glass throughout the centuries, for
Christian artists have never tired of portraying the great events that
carry the meaning of Christian existence. As the year passed, the
walls would tell the stories of the life of Jesus that had now become
the ongoing life of the church.

Nevertheless, another element has always been present in Christianity that transcends the yearly cycle—namely, the expectation of
the return of Jesus himself. Portrayals of Judgment Day and the
popularity of scenes from the Book of Revelation suggest that some-
day, perhaps soon, this world will end and a "new heaven and a new
earth" will be established by the hand of Christ himself. In the liturgy we find this in prayers—"Thy kingdom come!" in the Lord's
Prayer, for example—and in the interpretation of the Eucharist as
presaging a great banquet for the wedding of Christ and the church.
At times this different sense of time has broken through the bounds
of the regular, repeated ritual and exploded in millenarian movements (which, of course, Christianity itself was at the beginning).

Groups of Christians take on new and intense religious practices in preparation for the Second Coming, often ignoring the regular work of the church. The great spiritual movements of Christian history—the monastic movement of the fourth and fifth centuries, the Crusades and related movements of the eleventh, twelfth, and thirteenth centuries, the Reformation of the sixteenth and seventeenth centuries, and the evangelical awakenings of the nineteenth and twentieth centuries have all been accompanied by millenarian expectations. Christians begin to feel that the time is short, the work is coming to a close, and God will soon bring the perfect world they yearn for into being.

Some churches, though not fully millenarian, have taken an intermediate position in which they leave behind the church calendar, relying on another sense of time altogether. For example, the American Puritans eliminated all the feasts except Easter (they did not celebrate Christmas at all, regarding it as mostly pagan) and, of course, the regular Sunday services, which featured a lengthy sermon. Instead of the traditional feasts, their magistrates, on the advice of the ministers, would proclaim feast days or fast days whenever it seemed appropriate: a feast of thanksgiving when the community had experienced a blessing or a fast day when they experienced troubles, which, they believed, were due to their sins and therefore required penitence. Their faith in God's providence was so strong that they attributed to him sovereign power over each day, to choose whether he would administer blessing or curse. The community, the Puritans believed, should respond to God's immediate action rather than to a repetitive calendar. This was the way in which as a community they chose to imitate Christ: in full obedience to God the Father.

The church, then, has acted out the way of salvation in a variety of ways, in different modes of worship, in different responses to God's action in the temporal world. There is yet a third aspect to the church's work: the messianic task, to transform the world itself. In this dimension of Christian existence, being a successor to Christ means continuing the work he began of actually establishing God's kingdom. If one is looking toward Christ's immediate return, this impulse is likely to be weak. But often Christians have acted to organize and literally to govern the world in accord with the norms of the church itself. The Christian emperors of Byzantium, the popes of the Middle Ages, the radical reformers who wanted the "saints" to govern society, all expressed the confidence that Christianity is not merely waiting for the Messiah to return, nor is it only concerned with ensuring the salvation of its members; rather, it transforms the world by direct action. We find many examples of this impulse in modern times as well: Christian efforts to end the slave trade and free black slaves in the nineteenth century; temperance movements to control liquor consumption; Christian lobbies and political parties; Christian peace movements or nonviolent movements; campaigns for laws against abortion or homosexuality or in favor of prayer in the schools. Sometimes Christians appear politically liberal in these campaigns, sometimes conservative; but all express the conviction that the church has the duty to work toward the perfection of the world during this in-between time before Christ returns.

Thus the church in the various dimensions of its corporate life aims to be the body of Christ: as an organic entity with each of its members supporting the others and being supported; as an evangelistic organization, continuing the preaching of Jesus; as a keeper of the mysteries, re-enacting the redemptive sacrifice of Christ and extending the pattern of his life into the yearly round; as a vehicle of the Holy Spirit in all realms; and as the executor of Christ's will for the world, establishing the perfect kingdom of God on earth. These have been the great strengths of the church through the ages, and they have given direction and purpose to innumerable individual lives. Yet there is also a strong personal dimension to Christianity, suggesting to every individual that he or she also can live in imitation of Christ. Not only by participating in the great body of the church, but also by sanctifying his or her personal life in Christ, can the Christian achieve spiritual fulfillment.

Jesus as Model of the Christian's Personal Life

Christianity sanctifies the great events of a person's life by bringing them under the umbrella of Christian ideals. These events are marked in virtually all societies by rites of passage: birth, puberty, marriage, death. They are times of critical change in biological and/ or social status, and although modern American society has paid little attention to them, they are usually accompanied by profound

psychological transformations. Christianity, in its work of transforming human beings toward divinity, uses rituals around these
crucial events to aid in that process as well as to ease the transition
for the individual and the community.

Birth has attracted to it the rite of baptism and christening, a
modified version of confirmation. Though some churches shun infant baptism, many have used it as a means of confirming the infant
born into a Christian family as part of the organism of the church.
The purity of the infant corresponds to the purification of baptism,
so the two seem naturally to go together. Yet at the same time,
many churches have held that, despite the appearance of innocence,
the infant is already contaminated by original sin, transmitted down
through its ancestors ever since Adam, so baptism is already necessary in order for the child to be a part of the church. Christening
gives the child a Christian name: as Christ received his title, "the
Christ," or Messiah, so the child receives the proper name—traditionally, the name of a saint. By this too the child becomes a social
being in a Christian community of "saints."

Puberty has received surprisingly little attention considering that
most religious traditions focus sharply on that crucial period of transition from childhood to adulthood. It is not quite so surprising,
however, when we remember that puberty means the onset of adult
sexuality, and in Christianity sexuality has been regarded as one of
the great sources of sin. Most churches have interpreted the sin of
Adam and Eve as primarily sexual, a sin of lust (though some
churches have focused more on the sin of pride). The danger in sexuality has meant that puberty as a physical transformation has been
largely ignored, and privileges and responsibilities of adulthood
have been emphasized instead. Many churches have made the age of
puberty an appropriate time for confirmation: final acceptance into
the church as a full member. Also, to deal with rising sexual impulses, adolescents in earlier times were often encouraged to enter
religious orders, where they would be taught celibacy, or to marry
and be chaste within the marriage. Thus the taking of vows and
weddings have superseded puberty rites. Both of these are mar-
riages: in the religious order, one becomes married to Christ; in the
wedding, one unites with one's spouse "in Christ," imitating the
marriage of Christ to the church—an eternal, faithful union in
which each mirrors the other in holiness.

The rites of death in Christianity are designed to give comfort to the dying Christian; for, after all, he or she is going to an eternal life. In Roman Catholicism, for example, the rite of extreme unction offers the individual an opportunity for penitence, clearing the soul through a final confession, then for being anointed once again, as at confirmation, like the descent of the dove of purity on Jesus. Death is a summation of life, and it looks forward to the next. We find in some forms of evangelical Christianity an expectation that the dying person may even be able to see the brightness of the light ahead, may have a vision of future joy immediately before death. The Christian is usually buried on the third day, expressing the identification with Christ who was resurrected on the third day. Tombs are marked with empty crosses, not crucifixes, thus symbolizing the Resurrection: the soul of the person is no longer here.

Thus the major passages of the individual's life receive their distinctive Christian flavor, always pointing to Christ. More generally, however, the model of Jesus has stood out in the guides to personal piety through the ages as one that should be present in every moment of a person's life. Essentially, this has been a model of continual purification, leading toward sinlessness. Jesus was above all that human being who did not sin, who did not fall into temptation or error—for he was God. If human beings are to become like God, they must eliminate sin. This has required ritual, self-discipline, and continual self-examination in terms of Christian ideals.

Probably the most dramatic example of the process of purification has been the Roman Catholic rite of penance. Sometime in the second or early third century, churches began to exclude from the Eucharist those who had committed serious sins, at least for the period of Lent, sometimes for many years. Such persons requested admission to the order of penitents. They wore sackcloth and ashes or other special garments, sat in a separate section of the church, observed sexual continence, and devoted themselves to prayer and acts of charity. Some churches used public flogging or required penitents to prostrate themselves at the feet of the congregation. This series of rites, the early sacrament of penance, could be performed only once in a person's life. Afterward one would be restored to the church and thenceforward would live an upright and, it was hoped, perfect Christian life. Since it could be done only once, many people postponed it till late in life.

Penance acknowledges the quest for perfection in the face of the obvious fact that humans continue to be imperfect even after original sin is washed away; the phenomenon commonly known as "backsliding" is a universal occurrence. It is so widespread, in fact, that the churches found the original form of penance too strict. They had generally relaxed the punishments of penance by the fourth century, and in the sixth century a new form, introduced by Irish monks, spread through the churches. The sinner would have a private audience with a priest in which the priest, ideally without knowing the identity of the penitent, heard the sins that the sinner wished to confess and prescribed a correction, together with certain devotional acts, as a way of making amends in the person's relationship to God. This practice was repeatable. It became known as auricular confession, or simply confession. The acts prescribed tended to be positive practices, unlike the asceticism of earlier days. Fasting and self-flagellation were still modes of penance, but so were endowing masses (which gave financial support to the church), going on pilgrimage, and saying additional prayers and psalms.

In Protestantism confession became optional, a private matter, and any Christian could confess to any other. Occasionally, however, confession has risen again to become an important rite even in Protestant sects. The famous Shakers of the nineteenth century, led by Mother Ann Lee, practiced confession to the "saints," that is, the whole communal group, as a major ritual. More commonly, Protestants have substituted a process of self-examination, identifying and correcting one's own faults. Among the Puritans, such self-examination was a crucial part of the process of becoming a church member, and one did share it with one's pastor. However, the practice was not so much a confession of specific sins as a narrative account of the struggles of one's spiritual life. The importance of testimonials— that is, giving a public account of one's previous sinful life and one's experience of salvation—in some evangelical churches indicates the continuing presence of the same impulse; open examination of one's faults and errors is a crucial part of Christian spiritual development. In modern times, psychotherapy has often taken the place of self-examination and confession for Christians (and others) whose churches no longer provide a satisfactory ritual expression of that impulse.

The larger purpose of such rites is the purification of the soul, to abolish temptation to sin in order to live a more Christly life. What exactly was meant by the more Christly life has varied from one era to the next. At times the model has been an ascetic one, with the monk exemplifying the highest ideals. Jesus was conceived of as the one who left the world entirely behind—especially the worldly temptations of wealth, power, and sexual lust. Only the monk could fulfill this ideal, but people could take on part of it while living family lives and working in the world. They could, for example, practice charity, giving away their wealth rather than accumulating it; they could spend extra time in prayer and worship, focusing their attention on the godly rather than the everyday realm. They could for a period of time take on vows of continence, fast regularly, or even spend short periods of time in a monastery or convent. They could go on pilgrimages—becoming for some months or a year wanderers like Jesus, living off the gifts and hospitality of others, seeking only God. All these variants on the ascetic model of Jesus ordinary people could incorporate into their lives.

Another popular model of Jesus has emphasized more his inner character and ethical action than his ascetic life. Jesus was humble, kind, forgiving, charitable; outwardly he exemplified love toward his fellow human beings. This more humanized Jesus was drawn from sections of Scripture that told, for example, of his feeding the multitudes, forgiving the prostitute Mary Magdalene, calling the little children to him. The Sermon on the Mount ("Blessed are the poor ... the meek ...," etc.) emphasized his humility; his telling a rich man how hard it was to get into the kingdom of God echoed the vow of poverty. This ideal has often appealed more to the laity and has grown increasingly strong since the Protestant Reformation. In this respect, Christians can take on the model of the loving person rather than the inner struggles of the ascetic to attain godliness. Instead of the image of battling Satan in the wilderness, one finds the hymn "What a Friend We Have in Jesus."

Other portraits of Jesus have emerged at various times. We saw in an earlier section both Jesus the teacher of wisdom and Christ the king. Modern times have seen portraits of Jesus as social reformer, successful businessman, or revolutionary. The diversity of portrayals reflects the multiplicity of Christian communities and Christian ideals throughout history. The past century has seen scholars of early Christianity searching for the "historical Jesus" in an attempt to

Different models of Christ have appeared in art and statuary. Here "Christ gives Peter the Law," from a fourth century sarcophagus, suggests Christianity's connection with Judaism as well as Christ the teacher. Used by permission of Hirmer Archive, Munich. Below, the suffering Christ appears in Michelangelo's famous Duomo Pieta (Florence, Italy, mid-sixteenth century). Used by permission of SCALA/Art Resource, New York.

clarify who this person was, in the hope of constructing a firm model for the Christian life. The quest has not succeeded, however; the picture of Jesus in even the earliest Christian literature already was shaped by layers of tradition and the authors' own images of a holy man or Messiah. The amount that is incontestably authentic, if any, is too small and insignificant to build a rich model of human life.

Still, the ideal of Jesus continues to hold the imagination of Christians. He was the perfect man, the ideal of humanity (although some women in recent times have questioned whether the human ideal can be fully represented in a *male* figure). To rise above sin and error as Jesus did is, for Christians, to reach upward to God. Whether that means parting company with the material world as the ascetics did or becoming a loving person like the humanized Jesus, whether it means being impoverished or wealthy and charitable, it remains above the ordinary reach of life. To attain that ideal, to take on the *imitatio Christi*, requires continual self-examination, discipline, and practice. Whatever the specifics of the ideal, Christians have turned to the practice of purification of the soul to rise above ordinary human nature. Most Christian groups have held, of course, that this is not possible by human effort alone: God's grace, mediated through the saving acts of Christ's suffering, death, and resurrection, have made it truly possible to approach the divine life, the sinless life. Even when we look at human efforts to follow in Jesus' steps, we must remember that central assertion of the Christian myth: that God became man in order that human beings could return to God. For that remains Christianity's great mystery.

From reflection on their particular tradition and from their sense of the transformation that Christ brings to their lives, Christians in every era formulate their highest ideals. Christianity holds out the promise of bringing humans to the intersection of the divine and human worlds, where the spiritual and invisible touches the earthly and visible. In that encounter a new humanity takes shape—different for each place and time, affected by politics, economics, aesthetics, and the like—but a new vision of humanity nonetheless. In the next chapter we will look closely at the dynamics of such changes, in two widely separated examples.

CHAPTER IV

Dynamics of Christian Life

W e have looked at Christianity as a historically developing religion, in overview, and we have examined some of its principal enduring features. Both the history and the structures can better be understood, however, if we look at specific examples in greater depth. For Christianity at any given time, in any particular place, is *both* a defined community with a set of beliefs and ceremonies held to be the foundation of the tradition *and* a community changing its thoughts and practices to grapple with new situations. How this can be, how change and continuity can be simultaneously present, will become clear as we look at particular examples.

We will consider two cases, far removed from one another in space and time, and different in the kinds of source material they present for our consideration. The first is a ritual: the pilgrimage to Saint James (Santiago) of Compostela in Spain, as it developed in the twelfth century. The increasing popularity of this pilgrimage gave it the character of a mass movement, encouraged and guided by the elites of medieval Europe. Its story must be pieced together from fragments of legend, liturgy, and chronicle. The second example is a pair of biographies: those of Lyman Beecher and Harriet Beecher Stowe, father and daughter, from the nineteenth-century United States. They left a considerable body of written work and personal material from which we can reconstruct their lives and thoughts, and the historical details of the period are well known. Since they are closer in time to us, some of the issues their lives raised will be more familiar than those of the twelfth century. Yet we will also be able to see across the centuries some common themes in the struggles of Christians to come to terms with the problems of their times.

The Pilgrimage to Compostela

Pilgrimage itself has a long history in Christianity as well as in other religions. Undertaking a journey to visit a holy place—the grave of a saint, the site of some famous religious event—has been almost universally regarded as good for the soul. Whether it is to obtain a blessing, to pay homage to authority, or to be purified of one's past errors, going on pilgrimage is especially effective. The physical and psychological effort of leaving home uproots people from their old habits and familiar environment, and that in itself can spur changes in their personal lives. In addition, travel, in all ages and places until the past hundred and fifty years, was difficult, burdensome, and unpredictable. An ancient saying has it that travel diminishes one's wealth, one's fame, and one's fertility—an adage that in most cases probably held true. To take on a long and difficult journey, then, meant that one gave up a great deal of familiarity and comfort. Except for the rare lone adventurer, a person would have to feel considerable desire for change to enter upon a pilgrimage.

In Christian history, those who went on pilgrimage were generally regarded as pious souls—less than the martyrs or monks, but certainly devout men and women worthy of praise. The favorite sites were Jerusalem, where Jesus himself had walked and where the church had begun, and Rome, where according to tradition Peter and Paul had died martyrs' deaths and where the Western church had its highest seat. Throughout the centuries, devout Christians would travel to these holy spots to pray, ask forgiveness of sins, or seek nearness to God. Yet in the early centuries pilgrimage was a voluntary, private devotion, usually practiced only by those wealthy enough to afford the journey.

In the sixth century the Irish missionary monks who crisscrossed Europe began to impose pilgrimages as penance for certain sins, especially sins that were openly scandalous. Nobles or priests who were found to have committed some crime often were assigned long pilgrimages. Over the centuries this motive for pilgrimage increased in importance. By the twelfth century many undertook pilgrimage whether a priest had imposed it as punishment or not; they believed they had accumulated so many sins, or such great ones, that they needed to satisfy some of the punishment due them by an especially holy act. (By this time the church held that the guilt of sin was absolved through confession, but the punishment still had to be paid, usually in purgatory, after death.) In the same period, the doctrine of indulgences grew in importance; the pope through the bishop occasionally granted remission of part of the punishment to those who went on pilgrimage, those who gave alms, and/or those who were present at the consecration of a church. At first indulgences were few and far between and, in any case, remitted only a portion of the penalty. But from the late eleventh century onward, greater and more frequent indulgences were offered. The first certain record of a plenary indulgence—granting remission of all penalties for sin—was offered by Urban II in 1095 to participants in the First Crusade.

Thus pilgrimage moved from the periphery of Christian devotion to near the center as the Christians of Europe became more concerned about purging themselves of sin. It was just at this time that the pilgrimage to the Spanish shrine of Saint James grew in popularity, and we will look later at the connection between the two developments. First, however, we might ask how it was that this shrine was known at all. There is no mention in the New Testament of James in Spain; nor is there any other apparent reason for a shrine in the far northwest corner of that country. Rome and Jerusalem were the obvious goals for long pilgrimages, and if one needed a short trip, there were many holy churches scattered through the countryside of Europe.

The answer has many dimensions, but the most direct comes from the cult of relics. As we observed in Chapter II, people of the early Middle Ages defined their religiousness largely through devotion to relics. Relics were stolen, transported across land and sea, dug up, and invented. Whenever a new relic appeared or an old one was found in a new place, it attracted attention and prestige to a church or abbey; often it provided the site for a new pilgrimage. In the late eighth century Charlemagne's reforms forbade the addition of new saints to the roster while simultaneously requiring that every church altar have a holy relic. Thus any shift in the geography of holiness would necessitate finding an old saint to verify the power of a place.

This is precisely what happened at Compostela. We have no contemporary accounts of the discovery of the relics of Saint James. We do know that a legend circulated from at least the seventh century saying James had preached in Spain. By the early ninth century a cult of James had begun in northwest Spain. A later legend tells us the following story: A hermit named Pelayo,[8] together with some villagers and shepherds, noticed strange starlight and angelic voices in the vicinity of a wooded area. Pelayo informed the nearest bishop, Theodomir. He and his assistants fasted for three days, then searched the thick woods until they discovered a hut containing a marble sarcophagus. Inside rested the bones of Saint James (one version adds that an attached piece of parchment gave the full description of how the bones had arrived there). Theodomir told King Alfonso II, who immediately constructed a church on the site. This was the beginning of the cathedral of Compostela—which, in one derivation of the name, means *campus stellae*, "field of the star." From that time the legend of James in Spain grew, and the Christian kings of northern Spain held James to be the protector of the country.

Nevertheless, Compostela remained of mostly local importance until the eleventh century. Then Europe, in the middle of the spiritual revival led by Cluniac reformers and culminating in the Crusades, began to find in Spain an interesting focus of pilgrimage. We will shortly look at the reasons why. But first it is important to understand what a pilgrimage involved. It was not a matter simply of packing one's bags and taking the next wagon for Compostela. Becoming a pilgrim in the twelfth century meant taking on a serious religious obligation; it was almost like entering a religious order. Some traveled with the pilgrims for lighter reasons, to be sure— merchants to sell their wares, adventurers for the excitement of travel—but the true pilgrim was traveling to come closer to God.

The Route of the Pilgrim

Since pilgrims might be gone a long time, they would first set their affairs in order and make their wills. The latter was not a common practice—indeed, only pilgrims had the undisputed privilege of wills, of deciding how their property would be distributed in case of death. Then, whether going voluntarily or because of an imposed penance, the pilgrim would go to his or her priest to be confessed. The full confession of all sins was necessary before setting out on the

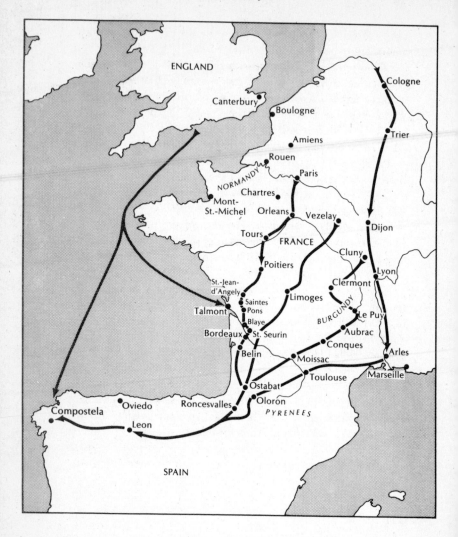

ENGLAND

Canterbury
Boulogne
Amiens
Rouen
Paris
NORMANDY
Chartres
Mont-
St.-Michel
Orleans
Vezelay
Tours
FRANCE
Cluny
Dijon
Cologne
Trier
Lyon
Poitiers
Clermont
Le Puy
St.-Jean-
d'Angely
Saintes
Pons
Limoges
BURGUNDY
Aubrac
Arles
Talmont
Blaye
Bordeaux
St. Seurin
Conques
Marseille
Belin
Moissac
Ostabat
Toulouse
Roncesvalles
Oloron
Compostela
Oviedo
Leon
PYRENEES

SPAIN

Routes to Compostela from France and England

holy journey that would satisfy some of the penalties. Pilgrims donned the symbols of their status: for men, a tunic (often marked with a cross), a staff, and a pouch for carrying valuables. These marked them, though unofficially, as religious personages, and would, it was hoped, attract alms and hospitality along the route. Pilgrims had to carry money for road tolls or religious donations, but otherwise they were expected to travel light, imitating the poverty of Jesus and relying on charity.

If they seemed materially impoverished, however, they could expect great spiritual richness. No matter which of the routes pilgrims took, they would be visiting the greatest and holiest spots of all Europe. For example, the pilgrim from Burgundy (eastern France) would go first to Cluny itself, which boasted relics of Saint Peter and Saint Paul. Next might be nearby Clermont, where Urban II preached the First Crusade and where the church of Notre Dame de Port had a famous tenth-century statue of Virgin and Child. Next would be Le Puy, an ancient pilgrimage center and possibly a holy site of the Druids in pre-Christian days. Famous for its volcanic craters as well as its thorn from Christ's crown, donated by Saint Louis, it had a special stone, the Pierre de Fièvres, on which the sick could lie while priests recited prayers to the Virgin. Next came the church of Sainte Foi at Conques, also a site of healing, especially for blindness and diseases of the eyes. It was well known that the monks of Conques had stolen the relics of Foi from another site, but this did not mar their holiness—after all, Foi would not have let herself be stolen if she had not wanted to move. Besides her own relics, including the famous crowned "Majesty," the church possessed the famous reliquary of King Pepin: a jeweled wooden chest containing relics of the Virgin and Saints Peter, Paul, Andrew, George, John the Evangelist, John the Baptist, Martin, and Hippolytus, plus the prepuce and umbilical cord of Jesus. Before reaching the Pyrenees, the pilgrim would also stop at Saint Peter of Moissac, a church believed to have been founded by King Clovis, the first Frankish convert.

A pilgrim from north-central France would come to Orleans, where at the cathedral of the Holy Cross could be seen a chalice consecrated by Jesus and a fragment of the cross. At Tours, the great basilica of Saint Martin contained relics of that saint, one of the patron saints of France. In Poitiers the pilgrim could visit the enshrined

Pilgrims frequently stopped along the route to pay homage to relics of famous saints. This bejeweled statue, 33½ inches high, stood atop the case said to contain relics of Sainte Foi, famous for her ability to heal the blind—hence the large, staring eyes. From the Abbey Treasure, Conques; photo used by permission of Maurice Babey, Basel.

remains of Bishop Hilary, a famous upholder of orthodoxy in battles with the heretics. Poitiers was also the scene of the famous battle against the Muslims in 732, which Charles Martel had won, preserving Gaul for Christianity. At Saint-Jean-d'Angély was the head of Saint John the Baptist; and there too the pilgrim could hear a great liturgical choir of a hundred monks singing day and night. At Saint Romain of Blaye there was the body of the famous knight Roland; at Saint Seurin of Bordeaux, Roland's horn; at Belin, the tomb of Roland's compatriots. These warriors had died in battles against the Basques on returning from the Crusade, but legend held that they had been fighting the Muslims. They were therefore treated as saints, martyrs in the cause of fighting the infidels.

There were other routes from different parts of France and from Italy, plus many other supplementary roads through famous towns like Chartres or Amiens. The northern routes converged at the approach to the Pyrenees, and the climb into the mountains marked a high point in more ways than one. There the pilgrims came together in large numbers for the final approach to the holy site. At the pass at Ostabat, each planted a small wooden cross, imitating the large stone one that, it was said, had been erected by Charlemagne himself. They went on to Roncesvalles, where they could see the huge rock Roland had split with his sword. At other towns there were more relics including those of the famous scholar Saint Isidore at Léon. Some might take a side trip to the church of San Salvador at Oviedo, where King Alfonso VI had revealed a great casket of holy relics. Then finally, after a lengthy trek in the semi-arid plain, they approached Compostela.

The pilgrims immersed themselves in a stream two miles outside the city, just as their counterparts in the Holy Land would bathe in the Jordan. This was almost a second baptism, an initiatory purification. Each person picked up a stone from the limestone quarry and carried it to the city, thus contributing his labor to the building of the shrine. Entering the city itself, the pilgrims would pass through streets filled with merchants and minstrels, stopping perhaps to buy. Eventually most pilgrims would purchase a scallop shell, the insignia of Compostela. Their main purpose now, however, would be to find lodgings and prepare to go to the basilica for services.

Most pilgrims would try to be at the church for an all-night vigil at least once during their stay. They would, of course, hear Mass in the church as often as possible, as they had in each church along the way. If possible, a pilgrim would have arranged the trip so as to be there on one of the feast days of Saint James, either July 25 or December 30. Then he or she could hear the great liturgy of the saint himself, which had developed by the twelfth century into a magnificent piece celebrating James and John as the "Sons of Thunder," called by Christ to do his work on earth. The glory of the processional the pilgrims would witness on one of the feast days was overwhelming:

The King marched wearing his crown and royal robes in the midst of his many knights accompanied by the different orders of his counts and commanders. He held in his right hand the silver scepter of the Spanish Empire, embellished with gold flowers of various workmanship and studded with variegated gems. The diadem on his forehead, with which he was crowned for the greater glory of the Apostle, was of

beaten gold, adorned with enameled flowers *niello*, precious stones
and glistening images of birds and four-footed creatures. An un-
sheathed two-edged sword, decorated with golden flowers and glistening inscription, with golden pommel and silver hilt, was borne before the King. At the head of the clergy, preceding the King, the
archbishop walked in dignity surrounded by the other bishops. He
was vested pontifically with a white mitre and gilded sandals and in
right hand, with white gloves and a gold ring, he held a crozier of
ivory. The clergy advancing before him were bedecked in venerable
ornaments, the 72 canons of Compostela were vested in begemmed
silken copes with silver brooches, gilded flowers, and everywhere re-
splendent fringes. Some wore silk dalmatics which were embroidered
in gold from the shoulder down and of exquisite beauty.

Others were adorned with golden necklaces studded with gems,
bands laced with gold, the richest mitres, attractive sandals, golden
cinctures, gold-embroidered stoles and maniples [armbands] inset
with pearls. What more is to be said? The clergy of the choir of Santiago displayed every kind of precious stones and as much silver and
gold as can be told. Some carried candlesticks and others silver cen-
sers; and others again crosses of silver-gilt. Some carried Gospel books
with variously begemmed golden covers, others coffers with the relics
of many saints; and other phylacteries [boxes inscribed with holy
words]. Finally others bore gold or ivory choir batons, their tips decorated with onyx, beryl, sapphire, carbuncle, emerald, or other gem.
Others bore two tables of silver-gilt on silver cars which held the light-
ed tapers offered by the faithful.

The splendid sights, illuminated by hundreds of candles, and the
sweet smells of incense must have been stunning to every pilgrim.
The songs proclaimed the glory of James:

O James, Apostle of Christ, unconquered soldier of the eternal king,
shining in the brilliant court of the apostles as the sun glittering amid
the stars, you gleam in glory.

The prayers appealed to James to pray for the poor pilgrims, and
guide them to salvation:

O helper of all the ages, glory of the Apostles, bright light of those
who live in Galicia, protector of pilgrims, James the uprooter of lies,

loosen the chains of our sins and lead us to the haven of salvation. You who assist those in peril who cry to you both on sea and land, help us now and in the danger of death, and lead us.[9]

Finally, after attending the morning service, the pilgrims grouped themselves around a priest, who would deliver to them the indulgences they had earned by making pilgrimage. They brought gifts of cash or jewelry to the altar, then venerated the relics of James—his chain, crown, hat, staff, knife, and stone. They then received the indulgence. They touched and kissed the saint's tomb, prayed earnestly there, and promised good works for the future. It was hoped they would also have the experience of feeling forgiven of their sins. After this, the rite of penance was complete. It was now that the pilgrims would buy scallop shells as the public sign of finishing the pilgrimage. Then, although they might tour the city, they were free to return home.

The Meaning of the Pilgrimage

From one point of view, the entire pilgrimage was a lengthy and elaborate preparation for the final purification, which took place when the pilgrim celebrated the divine service at the basilica and prayed at the saint's tomb. Such a description would hardly do it justice, however: sins could be forgiven and a life mended at any church. Why the multiplication of visits to churches and holy sites all along the way? Why the appeal to a distant saint like James rather than one close to home? A long journey might be a catalyst for change and renewal of one's life, but how are we to understand the elaborate ritual of the journey?

It might seem simply a yearning for greater holiness, expressed quantitatively: if one Mass is good, twenty are better. But that would miss the special quality of medieval piety. In fact, to the eyes of the pilgrim, each locus of holiness had its own special quality: the healing of fevers at Le Puy was different from the healing of blindness at Conques; the piety of John the Evangelist was different from that of Hilary the bishop. Christian holiness in that age was polymorphous; it had many facets, each of which could be touched in different places.

There were, of course, recurrent themes, and sometimes a pilgrimage route emphasized certain kinds of holiness more than others. That was certainly true in the case of Compostela. The legends recounted to the travelers on these routes spoke often about the warrior heroes: Charlemagne, Roland and his knights, Charles Martel, King Clovis. Part of this was nationalistic history and legend, integrated into the Christian framework. But part of it was new or newly popular, and it took on special significance in the context of the times. The story that Roland had battled the Saracens rather than the Basques is an example. For the Muslims were figures of great contemporary significance; crusades had begun to oust the infidels from the Holy Land, and Spain itself had long been the site of such conflict. Since the 800s, much of Spain had been under Muslim control, and Christians were struggling to regain territory. In 997 Christian armies had suffered terrible defeats at the hands of Almanzor, who had devastated northern Spain and razed Compostela itself. Afterward his kingdom fell apart in the hands of weaker heirs, and northern Spain rose again with the aid of the French. In this context, we can see Saint James connected with the rise of medieval martial spirit.

The early stories of James, son of Zebedee, mentioned his nearness to Jesus; he was a brother of John the Evangelist. Some spoke of his preaching in Spain and the translation of his bones to Galicia in northwestern Spain. Later legends, however, viewed him as Matamoros, Moor-Slayer (killer of Muslims). A twelfth-century legend told the story of the battle of Clavijo, supposedly in 845, when Christian forces under King Ramiro were hard pressed by the Muslims. In a dream, Saint James appeared to the king promising victory. When he told his warriors, they prayed together and then rushed on the enemy. In the sky at the head of the Christian legions appeared the Apostle James in shining armor, on a white horse, carrying a white banner with a blood red cross. He himself, said the legend, killed sixty thousand Moors. Afterward the army vowed that all Spain would pay tribute to Compostela.

The battle of Clavijo is fictitious; it was probably a reflection in legend of a later battle, in 939 under Ramiro II, the story of which was made famous in many chronicles of the time. It too was a battle by Christians of northern Spain against Muslims, where James appeared, together with another saint, riding a white horse into battle;

it too resulted in a vow of tribute to Compostela. In either case, however, we find James linked with a military and nationalistic spirit, as Christians rose up against Islamic invaders. After the devastation wrought by Almanzor, James's prestige may have waned somewhat. But in the 1060s his legend rose again, and it was claimed that he helped King Ferdinand I and his famous warrior Rodrigo Diaz de Bivar—later known as El Cid—win the battle of Coimbra.

By the late eleventh century, then, Spain, Saint James, and the pilgrimage were linked in a particular set of legends that told, not only of James's great piety and closeness to Jesus, but also of his being an ally in Christian warfare. The next stage of development occurred under Alfonso VI, one of the sons of Ferdinand. Alfonso took a company of clergy and knights to the town of Oviedo, whose cathedral of San Salvador, since the beginning of the tenth century, had occupied a place of honor second only to Compostela. The church possessed a case of relics that no one dared to examine, for in 1030 some clergy had opened it and been struck blind by the dazzling light that burst out. Alfonso and his cadre fasted and did penance in preparation, and on the fourth Friday of Lent they opened it and saw what they claimed were fragments of the cross, drops of Jesus' blood, the napkin that had bound his head, crumbs of the Last Supper, and relics of Mary and the apostles. This ceremony became famous all over Europe, adding to Alfonso's prestige. He was confident enough to declare himself emperor of all Spain—in the same year that the reforming Pope Gregory VII (Hildebrand) declared that Spain was a province of the church.

The scene was set for a struggle between national pride and the universal church, and the outcome would deeply affect the pilgrimage to Compostela. Many of the Christians in Spain asserted their unique tradition over against the pope in a struggle over ritual. The ancient Visigothic church had developed a liturgy, called the Mozarabic rite, that was significantly different from the Roman. Alfonso VI, however, decided not to be narrowly nationalistic. Married to a French woman, Constance, the daughter of the duke of Burgundy, he was drawn to the universal church. He did not, therefore, use his prestige to support the Mozarabic partisans but chose to seek the aid of the monks of Cluny to popularize the pilgrimage to Compostela and thereby elevate Spain's role in the universal church. The men from Cluny were, as we saw in Chapter II, the great reformers and centralizers of the church, cementing the spiritual and political connections between France and Rome.

Now, as the twelfth century began, Cluny and the French extended their influence into Spain, once even putting a Cluniac monk into the archbishopric of Compostela. They were creating lasting connections between Spain, France, and Rome and, by extension, the whole church of Europe. The medium for this task of unification was the pilgrimage to Compostela. The work that most exalted the pilgrimage was the *Book of St. James*, attributed to Pope Calixtus but actually written, probably around 1130, by a monk or monks from Cluny. The book told the stories of James, the miraculous transport of his bones, their discovery in Galicia, and the miracles that had happened by James's intervention. Most significantly, however, the book also recounted the story of Charlemagne, his great archbishop Turpin, and the famous warrior Roland. The popular *Chanson de Roland*, as well as earlier legends, had already celebrated the saintliness of Charlemagne, and the fair Roland had become one of the great medieval heroes. The legend as rewritten by Cluny now made Charlemagne the first pilgrim to Saint James: in a vision he was instructed to lead an army into Galicia and capture the road that led to Saint James's tomb, whereupon he went beyond Compostela to the sea and met the miraculous boat carrying the body of James from the Holy Land. In other expeditions, he conquered more of Spain for the Holy Roman Empire, but the third time his rear guard was attacked by Saracens, and Roland and his knights were slain.

The transformation of the legends of Charlemagne and Roland reflected and enhanced the transformation of piety that centered on the pilgrimage to Compostela. James in Spanish legend had been a Christian knight, fighting with those who wanted to maintain Christianity in Spain against the Muslim onslaught. He could have remained merely a local hero, but the alliance of Spanish royalty with Cluny to promote the pilgrimage gave him a larger role: he was the perfect figure to rouse the spirit of all of Christian Europe in the age of the Crusades. Cluny's effect on the spirituality of Europe was manifold: it upheld the monastic way of life as the true channel for proper devotion to God; it elaborated the liturgy as the pure expression of that devotion; it brought penance to the center of the Christian life even for laymen; and it taught the knights a religious discipline by focusing their martial energies on the infidels. In the last task, the pilgrimage to Compostela served a dual purpose: it brought the pilgrim to the very border of a Muslim country, just as in the Holy Land, and it also brought him or her to the place where the spirit of holy war reigned supreme, the Tomb of Saint James. Moreover, at each step of the way, the relics of the saints, Mary, and Jesus were intertwined with the heroes of war. Paradoxically, the penance that stemmed from the humility of encountering the most holy relics was mixed with the cultivation of heroic temperament from touching the bones of Roland or the stone cross of Charlemagne.

We can see from this example that the practice of a ritual may have many dimensions other than the most obvious. Pilgrimage as an expression of devotion and means of purification has had a long and venerable history in Christianity; the pilgrimage to Saint James was a part of that tradition. Yet it was also much more. It grew out of the evolving spirit of the "church militant"—from the Spanish resistance to Muslim rule to the crusading spirit of the eleventh and twelfth centuries. For reasons that may remain obscure, James became the focus of Spanish resistance legends, and this in turn made him the perfect vehicle for the growing militance of the knights. Further, although Spain claimed him as a national saint, he was, like Peter and Paul, intimately connected to the church universal. He could reflect Spain's ties to Rome and be appropriated by the French monks of Cluny as a symbol for all Christians in their battles against the infidel. Finally, he could be for the pilgrim a focus of penance and humility and, at the same time, a model of the heroic warrior who was the exemplary figure of the age.

The story of the Saint James pilgrimage shows how a ritual ancient in its heritage and familiar in its form can be adapted to express the spirit of a particular time and place, even the political attitudes and dreams of particular groups of people. In the next section, we will examine how Christian symbols and beliefs underwent cultural change in another context.

Lyman Beecher and Harriet Beecher Stowe

The Beecher family was one of America's most famous families. Like the Adamses in politics and the Jameses in literature and philosophy, they made their mark in religion and culture. The

Beechers' influence reached far, partly because there were so many of them. Lyman had three wives in succession, the first two bearing him eleven children who lived to adulthood. Of these, five achieved wide renown: Catharine was a pioneer in women's higher education; Edward, a minister and editor, became a college president; Harriet wrote popular stories and novels; Henry Ward was a nationally known minister; and Isabella was involved in the campaign for women's rights. Even some of the lesser known had significant achievements. William, the oldest male, was a minister in a number of cities; Charles, an influential liberal minister, became superintendent of public instruction in Florida and demanded higher education for blacks; Thomas, another minister, led his community in Elmira, New York, to break new ground in dealing with urban problems. Of the women, only Mary lived a wholly private life. George died at the age of thirty-four of a gunshot wound. James served as a minister for many years but suffered from poor health after being wounded in the Civil War in his thirties.

Of such a large and illustrious family, a father such as Lyman Beecher, himself a famous minister, could be rightly proud. And indeed he was; yet he was also greatly concerned for his family, for none of his children embraced the religion he preached: the traditional Calvinist creed. This makes the Beechers doubly interesting; not only can we study a large Christian family through their public writings and private letters, but we can also see within the boundaries of the family itself some of the dynamics of religious change. Since we cannot look in a few brief pages at the entire family, we will focus on Lyman and his third daughter, the sixth surviving child, Harriet. Lyman often said that Harriet was so bright and interesting, he wished she had been a boy. That set the tone for their relationship: a deep interest, pride, and love, but also the distance that in the nineteenth century could not be bridged between the world of men and the world of women.

The World of Lyman Beecher

Lyman wanted his sons to follow in his footsteps, to become ministers of the gospel (they all did), for religion was his ruling passion. He came from a heritage and a region—he was a seventh-generation New Englander—that still in 1800 could be called Puritan. Puritan did not mean and should never have meant "puritanical," that is, prudish about the personal vices of drink, sex, dancing, and the like (the proper adjective for that would be *Victorian*). Puritan did mean having a strong sense of religion and morality at the center of personal and social life. The church, generally Congregational or Presbyterian, was at the center of society, influencing government and regulating the behavior of citizens. Church attendance was a major part of one's duty to God and an important way of becoming learned in the faith, for the minister's sermons were erudite and carefully argued from Scripture and reason. Every intelligent man was expected to participate in theological discussions, and women as well read treatises on God's providence, the nature of free will, or human depravity. Regular social occasions included afternoon tea, where the subject might be the previous Sunday's sermons.

Each Puritan underwent a process of self-examination and personal experience of God's grace before conversion, that is, before being accepted as a full member of the church. This was the inward part of Puritan piety, besides the outward devotion to the church, reverence to ministers, and upright moral behavior. Conversion began with a sense of **conviction** of sin, the intense recognition of oneself as truly a sinner. Then, over a stretch of time, often several years, the awakened sinner examined his or her heart, intentions, behavior, and relation to God to see whether he or she might have any hope of salvation. In a theological system like Calvinism, all was predestined by God, but one could never know for sure one's future fate. Nevertheless, if one was sufficiently humble and received some signs of grace, of closeness to God, one might have hope of heaven after death. Men and women searched their souls in torment and eagerness, working to remove their sins, erase their self-deceit and pride, and put all their trust in God. Under the guidance of a minister, they analyzed their experiences, and if they and he felt that there were evidences of grace, they could be counted as converted—for this was the most one could know on earth about one's possibilities for salvation.

Lyman Beecher believed fully in this system. The sovereignty of God and his mysterious grace were pillars of his personal piety. Born in 1775 to a line of New Haven blacksmiths, he had forged his faith out of his own personal experience and learning. His father loved the world of ideas, but the only books in his aunt and uncle's home, where he actually grew up, were a Bible and a psalm book. His urge for learning and dislike of farm work motivated him to prepare for college, and he went to Yale. There he encountered the first challenges to his Christian faith in the thought of Thomas Paine, a deist, whose works the students were excitedly discussing. By the time he finished his studies and was ordained in 1798, he was already a fighter for Calvinist orthodoxy.

Beecher made a name for himself over the next thirty years as a champion of orthodox religion and morality over deism, freethinking, and Unitarianism. These rational forms of religion (to him irreligion) often denied the miracles of Jesus and diminished religion to those universal truths with which the reasoning mind could agree. To him, they denied God's great power and mystery. Moreover, he believed that their influence on the country was dangerous. Beecher feared that if people's sense of the sovereignty of God disappeared, if human beings thought they could decide what was true religion apart from what God had revealed, morals would decline and society would disintegrate. This, he thought, was what had happened with the French Revolution, in which liberal thinkers had wielded great influence.

In one of his most famous sermons, "A Reformation of Morals Practicable and Indispensable," Beecher argued that the only hope for the country was to return to the faith, laws, and institutions of the Puritan fathers. Even in his beloved Connecticut he saw signs of moral decline:

> Drunkards reel through the streets, day after day, and year after year, with entire impunity. Profane swearing is heard, and even by magistrates, as though they heard it not. Efforts to stop traveling on the Sabbath have, in all places, become feeble, and in many places. . . . they have wholly ceased. Grand jurors complain that magistrates will not regard their informations, and that the public sentiment will not bear them out in executing the laws. And conscientious men, who dare not violate an oath, have begun to refuse the office.[10]

The great society that the Puritans had built had kept this unrighteous behavior under control; now the controls were loosening, and human nature—with all its depravity, its urge to sinfulness—was creating moral devastation in the land. Lyman proposed several steps to correct the problems. First, the gospel ministers must call people's attention to the declining state of affairs. Then the better people in the community must take care to reform themselves. Attention should be directed to the education of the young and discipline within the family. Further, the existing laws against immorality must be enforced. Voluntary associations of citizens should form to pressure the magistrates to enforce the laws. Finally, the connection between sin and shame must be restored: the sinner must not be allowed to feel the approval or neutrality of his or her fellow citizens; on the contrary, they should express their disapproval so that the sinner might feel shame.

This was Lyman Beecher's call to the people of Connecticut, New England, and all the states to return to the ways of the civilization built by the founders of New England. Yet already in 1812 when he preached the sermon, the last pillars of that older society were shaking. Liberals and dissenting churches had begun to campaign for the separation of church and state in Connecticut and Massachusetts, the last fortresses of New England. Most other states in the new union had already disestablished their churches and proclaimed religious tolerance, but Connecticut and Massachusetts still held to the principle that the state should support religion. Taxes in these states went to support Congregational ministers, churches, and schools. Naturally enough, Lyman Beecher fought for the Standing Order, as it was called, the tradition of a connection between faithful Christianity and righteous government, but in 1818 Connecticut abolished state support of any church.

Surprisingly, after a brief period of dismay, Beecher changed his mind about seeing the event as a disaster. Soon he was saying that the separation of church and state was a good thing, for now people would have to come voluntarily to the church and would support it for heartfelt reasons rather than because of external pressures. He was in many respects right. Over the next twenty years, revivals and movements of moral reform—based on the voluntary associations Lyman had promoted—revealed the passion Americans could generate for their religion, and the evangelical churches grew successfully. But the change also meant subtle pressures on Calvinist theology. Society was no longer organized to execute God's commands, so that people should search their hearts to discover whether they were saved, whether they could enter society as full and upright Christians. Instead churches urged people to *seek* their salvation: religion appeared to be more a matter of the free agency of the individual.

This development would put Beecher in the middle of an interesting debate, one that signaled the coming changes in American Protestantism. Beecher was already considered a partisan of the "new divinity," a slight adaptation of Calvinist theology that allowed some room for human free will. God was sovereign and had predestined each soul, and human beings were depraved sinners who without grace could do nothing—yet God in his grace had made it possible for them to make some moves toward him. As he put it in his sermon on the reformation of morals, "The kingdom of God is a kingdom of means, and though the excellency of the power belongs to him exclusively, human instrumentality is indispensable."[11] Conservatives, or Old School Presbyterians, found this allowed too much. At the same time, more liberal ministers were emerging, such as the great revivalist Charles Grandison Finney, who allowed much more room for the free will of human beings in seeking salvation. Beecher would find himself attacked by Finney in the late 1820s for his conservatism and tried for heresy in the 1830s for his liberalism.

Nevertheless, Beecher was a man of battle, especially of moral and theological battle, and these opponents did not deter him. More important things remained for him: his great passion was still the moral state of American society. After all, he was a child of the American Revolution; he had grown up immersed in the passion of his contemporaries for the great cause of the United States as a new, free, and even holy, nation. By 1830 he saw the evangelical cause fairly well established in the eastern United States, but as he looked to the expanding West he became concerned again. In a famous essay, "Plea for the West" (1835), he described the land west of the Appalachians as full of promise, yet so untamed, so large, that it seemed as though nothing could govern it. Yet, he said, it was clear that men would control it, and the West in turn would affect the older part of the nation. Therefore the challenge was to tame the West in accord with the great traditions of the East. The great danger, as he saw it, was that Roman Catholic European immigrants and missionaries were moving rapidly into western cities and might soon dominate them, bringing with them all the flaws of European culture and the tryanny, as he saw it, of Roman Catholicism. Protestants must therefore move to the West, build up institutions of education, and thereby train westerners to govern themselves as a free, devout, and moral people.

When Lyman wrote this piece he was already practicing whatahe preached. In 1832, at the age of fifty-six, he had moved himself and many of his family (even though they were mostly grown) to the heartland of the new West, Cincinnati. There he had been invited to establish Lane Seminary, a school to train orthodox ministers who would bring a faithful religious influence to the chaotic frontier. This became Beecher's last great venture. It had many difficulties: in the second year of its operation, a class entered made up of many radical thinkers, led by Theodore Weld, a convert of Finney's. The group made abolition of slavery the chief issue facing the seminary, splitting the faculty and arousing the whole city—for Cincinnatians, though part of a free state, had many exchanges and cordial relations with slaveholders in Kentucky. Eventually the radicals departed to found a new school, Oberlin, in the north of Ohio. Beecher and the trustees were left with a damaged reputation among conservatives and had to search for funds to support the school and students to attend it.

The school did not fail while Beecher remained its president, but he gave it his last fruitful years. In 1846 another controversy arose: some of Lyman's opponents brought him to trial for improperly holding the presidency of Lane, an Old School seminary, when he was a New School Presbyterian (the two branches had officially split in 1835). Lyman won the case on the grounds that he could not be held responsible for the split in the denomination, and he had already been proved free of heresy. But the trial was taxing, and it clearly revealed the slippage of support for him at the seminary. In 1851, at the age of seventy-five, he resigned and returned to the East. The next twelve years were spent in gradual decline: he gathered his papers and occasionally preached, but his mind was no longer as keen as it once had been. He died in 1863.

The Christianity that Lyman represented can be summarized best not in terms of doctrine, even though that was often his field of battle, but in terms of values. Above all he held to a strong faith in a sovereign God whose gracious providence ruled all and a belief in the power of religion as transformative in people's lives. Equally important, however, was a belief in the importance of a society's relationship to God. The influence of religion in society, in the life of the nation, was as important as in the life of the individual; the nation needed righteous laws, righteous governors, and a responsible citizenry in order to stay on the right path. The soundest course, in Lyman's thought, was adherence to the proven tradition (namely, that of New England), combined with education, discussion, debate—in short, the use of reason and common sense—to produce a learned citizenry grounded in the heritage of the past. These were the best means of establishing religion and morals in the hearts and minds of people and in the society as a whole. To that end, the church, the ministry, and the seminary were absolutely central institutions, crucial to the health of American civilization as a whole. Lyman Beecher had a clear vision, then, of society—its ideal state, the dangers that threatened it, and the means to improve it—and a clear sense of the role of Christianity. It was that vision that guided him in New England and the West in struggling for the perfect society, the society that, he hoped, the United States was destined to achieve.

Lyman's children grew up in a home imbued with these values and energized by his passion for perfection. The atmosphere of the home, one of them once wrote, was charged with a kind of "moral oxygen" that made it exciting and stimulating virtually all the time. The practices of the family—daily prayers, churchgoing, learned theological discussions lasting long into the night—made the religion of Lyman a lived reality. Also, his great concern as a father for the fate of their souls came home to them at an early age, and sometimes weighed heavily on them. Yet, though they sustained some of his values, they all rejected traditional Calvinism and shaped different religious perspectives for themselves, even when they stayed within the framework of the established churches, as many of them did. Their changes reflected and shaped the ongoing transformation of American religion in the nineteenth century.

Harriet Beecher Stowe

Born in 1811, the sixth of Lyman Beecher's surviving children, Harriet felt somewhat obscure beside her older brothers and sisters.

Yet she also attracted the interest of her father with her bright intelligence and her writing ability. As early as the age of seven she was receiving attention from her teachers for her written work. At twelve, competing in a school essay contest, she won first prize and the praise of her surprised father. As she grew up, Harriet was an avid reader, of both the theological works in her father's library and, increasingly, the romantic literature coming from England—Lord Byron and Sir Walter Scott were among those permitted by her father—and from women writers. When she was not busy with teaching in her sister Catharine's school, she experimented with stories and poems on her own. Neither her father nor Catharine much encouraged her, however, for such work seemed frivolous compared to her other duties.

Meanwhile, in religion she seemed at first to stay close to tradition. She felt she had experienced conversion in early adolescence, and her account of it seemed to satisfy her father. But when she applied for membership in the church in Hartford, where she attended school, the minister questioned her so deeply as to arouse her doubts: if the whole universe were destroyed, he asked, would you be happy with God alone? She spent the next few years in doubt, sometimes experiencing morbid moods that may have been connected to religious questioning. This, indeed, would be natural in the Puritan tradition. But Harriet never brought this process to a resolution through a traditional conversion; she simply left it behind gradually. She married a man firmly in the tradition: Calvin Stowe, a professor at Lane Seminary in Cincinnati and a Bible scholar of the first rank. Despite his traditionalism, however, he had the curious faculty of falling into trance and experiencing visions from time to time.

Harriet married Stowe in 1836 at the age of twenty-five, and bore seven children (beginning with twins) over the next fourteen years, of whom all but one survived past childhood. She was devoted to her children, yet she also wanted to write. In that desire Calvin supported her, so she wrote stories and magazine articles, often staying up late at night to work on them. From the early 1840s onward, she was publishing regularly and supplementing her husband's meager income as a seminary teacher. By the late 1840s she had begun writing some antislavery essays. In 1850 the Stowes moved to Maine, where Calvin was to teach at Bowdoin College. Harriet had never liked Cincinnati, so she was delighted to return to the

East—and most of the other Beechers were back there too, with her
father soon to follow in 1851. Harriet had even greater energy for
writing after her last child was born in 1850.

Meanwhile, the controversy over slavery reached fever pitch with
the congressional debate over the great Compromise of 1850 which
proposed to admit California as a free state, and New Mexico and
Utah with the question open to decision by popular vote. Several
Beechers, including Henry Ward who was always a strong influence
on Harriet, were speaking out against slavery. Henry even brought a
runaway slave into his pulpit and raised, on the spot, the money to
buy his freedom. Harriet wrote a small piece of antislavery fiction
for the *National Era*, whose editor immediately invited her to contribute more of the same. She came up against a blank wall, however: she could not seem to write anything more. Then, in February
1851 while at Communion services, she received what she later saw
as her great inspiration: a vision of an aged black slave being beaten
mercilessly by his white overseer while another white man egged
him on and then a vision of the same black man praying that God
forgive his tormentors. She wrote down what she saw, and then the
ideas started to flow. She decided to write a novel, which she would
submit in serial form to the *National Era*. This was the beginning of
the work that made her famous: *Uncle Tom's Cabin*, one of the great
nineteenth-century American novels and one of the most popular
books ever published. Published in book form in 1852, it sold three
thousand copies the first day and three hundred fifty thousand in
less than a year in the United States. Within two years it was published in seventeen other languages. Over the next fifty-eight years it
sold between three and four million copies in the United States, one
and a half million in Britain, and four million in other languages.

The power of the novel lay in Harriet's expression of a great moral vision. She portrayed in vivid detail slaves, hopeful, suffering, or
rebellious; slaveholders and slave traders, some of them evil in nature, some feeling trapped helplessly in the system; operators of the
"underground railroad" who risked their lives and reputations to
save slaves; and above all, families, North and South, slave and free,
showing how everyone was affected by the damaging effects of the
institution of slavery. All who were touched by slavery felt suffering,
loss, pain, grief; only those who had the moral courage to fight it
could find some satisfaction. At the same time, the most dramatic

characters in the book were not the rebels but those who most exemplified self-sacrificing Christian love: Uncle Tom, the aged slave she had seen in her vision, and little Eva, delicate child of a Southern gentleman, who died with prayers for everyone on her lips.

We can see in these figures something of Harriet's transformation of her father's religious vision. In place of the anxiety-ridden converts of Puritanism, we find soulful human beings, so close to God in their very nature that they have no doubts, living constantly the life of love for their fellow human beings. On the other hand, we find a vision of society as intense and clear as Lyman's, a society guided by moral passion and devotion to the cause of purging its sins. Yet where Lyman's guidelines were the laws and institutions of tradition, Harriet's were the sanctity of the home and the strength of love in the family. Hers was a feminized vision, in which women and children provided the deep religious grounding of society, in which the life of feeling was a surer guide than the exercise of reason and argument. Judging from the popularity of her book, many American readers were moved by such a vision.

Harriet herself explored this area consciously and directly in another work, *The Minister's Wooing* (1859), which many regard as one of her best works. Its theme is the exploration of the ground of true religion, set in terms of a love triangle. Dr. Samuel Hopkins, the middle-aged minister who clearly represents Lyman Beecher, falls in love with young Mary Scudder, a spiritual young woman of good New England upbringing. However, Mary already loves James Marvyn, an adventurous and irreligious young man who becomes a sailor. James is lost at sea until late in the story when he returns, a converted Christian, on the eve of the wedding of Dr. Hopkins and Mary. Mary probably is a composite of Harriet's ideas of herself as a young girl and of her mother, who died when she was four. Thus the relationship between Mary, Hopkins, and James explores Harriet's own turn away from her father's religion, her attempt to find her own Christian way, and her attraction to the world of adventure—which she tames rather casually by making James a convert to Christianity.

The character of Mary is intensely feminine and spiritual: she was, Harriet says, "predisposed to moral and religious exaltation. Had she been born in Italy, . . . she might have seen beatific visions in the sunset skies." But as a child of New England, instead of lying "in mysterious raptures at the foot of altars, she read and pondered treatises on the Will." However, as she read or listened to Dr. Hopkins, she did not absorb information with the intellect alone. "Womanlike, she felt the subtle poetry of these sublime abstractions, . . . often comprehending through an ethereal clearness of nature what he had laboriously and heavily reasoned out." Hopkins, on the other hand, was the ideal righteous Christian man of Puritan times: humble, sincere, unselfconscious. He had in him "a perfect logic of life; his minutest deeds were the true results of his sublimest principles." He was not unemotional, but analysis prevailed: "Love, gratitude, reverence, benevolence—which all moved in mighty tides in his soul—were all compelled to pause midway while he rubbed up his optical instruments to see if they were rising in right order."[12] Ultimately, however, his great discipline had to face the test of passion. When James returned and a gossipy neighbor informed Hopkins that Mary and James had long loved each other, he had a great struggle to subdue his desires, to sacrifice his own happiness for theirs. Mary, for her part, was struggling to decide whether to keep her promise to the doctor or to tell him of her love for James; thanks to the intervention of the neighbor, she never had to make that decision.

Indeed, Harriet portrays the doctor's high ideals, his willingness to sacrifice "happiness" for "blessedness," as she puts it, as saving the situation. Mary is caught between her strong sense of duty and her deep passion for James, over which she has no control. Her own resolution comes only in her faith: that life is merely transient, that beyond the grave there is a future life, and love, which is immortal, will survive. She and James, in short, will be able to love each other after death, forever. She too would have sacrificed her earthly desires on behalf of her moral commitment, hoping for a future blessedness and happiness. Harriet clearly saw the struggle, accepted its dilemmas, and—though she gave her story a happy ending—recognized that often in this life there was no ideal resolution. One had to be true both to moral commitment and to one's deep feelings. Puritan tradition violated the feelings while upholding commitment; secular life threatened to lose the moral sense altogether. Harriet wanted both.

The outcome of the struggle for Harriet was that in 1864 she joined the Episcopal church. In this she followed her sister Catharine and her own twin daughters. Calvin's retirement from teaching at Andover Theological Seminary made the transition easier, as did Lyman's death in 1863. In a sense, Harriet was returning to her mother, Roxana, who was of Episcopal background. Though she barely knew her, she cherished her memory and the stories she heard from her older siblings. For Harriet the Episcopal church had a warmth and softness that the Puritan tradition lacked. She could express in it her appreciation for Catholicism, which had grown during her travels in Europe in the 1850s and 1860s—an appreciation that her father could not have understood. Her new religion allowed for gradual growth in spirituality for those who chose such a path, the slow refinement of the soul climbing the ladder to God. The strenuous way of her father's tradition, as she saw it, was powerful in its discipline but left too many behind floundering in despair. Thus she freed herself to move to a church more of her own leanings. The aesthetic richness of the liturgy and the connection to a more congenial devotional tradition could combine with the Protestant spirit of free inquiry, flexible authority, and the centrality of the believer's relationship to God.

Harriet spent the successful years of her life writing vigorously and traveling, usually to England and Europe, where she made contact with many of the leading literary lights. She wrote several more major works, the best being her novels of New England, and a large number of small pieces, publishing well into the 1870s. By 1880, however, her writing career was virtually at an end. She, like her father before her, spent her last years in quietude. Harriet died in 1896 and is still remembered as one of the century's great popular writers.

American Protestantism in a New Generation

Perhaps no generation between the Reformation and very recent times saw such dramatic religious change as that between Lyman Beecher's coming of age and that of his children. A number of writers have marked the year 1850 as a watershed in American religion, dividing the era of Calvinist tradition from the era of evangelical piety. This was precisely the time when Harriet Beecher Stowe and others of the Beecher clan were coming into their prime, while their father was retiring from active life. To be sure, there were agents of change before 1850: the growth of Methodism, the frontier revivals, the new revivalism of Charles G. Finney and others. But the issues concerning revivals were defined in Calvinist terms, though the new thinkers did not give Calvinist answers. After midcentury among the rising white middle class, the import of the old theological issues declined dramatically. Religion itself was being redefined.

Some have called the new evangelicalism sentimental—as indeed it was, some of the time. A better way of understanding it, however, is to say that the religious approach of the young Beechers and their contemporaries was rooted in feeling and sensibility rather than intellect and argument. The two generations shared an emphasis on moral character; but whereas the earlier generation saw character as the result of a rightly formed will, disciplined through careful education and the institutions of piety and law, the later generation saw character as a matter of proper feeling and sensitivity, shaped by loving nurturance and Christian friendship and association. The earlier aimed at clarity of thought and a vision of order, the later modeled itself after ideal figures of the imagination. That is why fiction, which was anathema to eighteenth-century Puritans, could become a vehicle of religion in the late nineteenth century. That is why Lyman argued for a reformation of morals in careful step-by-step reasoning, whereas Harriet portrayed characters who represented moral forces. In her world, dogma and argument could no longer teach well or engage people's support.

Lyman Beecher spoke of the government of God and urged his countrymen to preserve religion as the safeguard of the people. Harriet Beecher Stowe, never long doubting the government of God or the necessity of religion in American civilization, took issue with the mode of spirituality her father represented. For her, the moral character of the nation had to be ensured, not by preserving old laws and institutions, but by guarding the home and family and looking to the deep, feminine sensibility within to find guidelines for right action. Ultimately, she turned from her father's sense of right government to her mother's love and warmth and made self-sacrificing love the pivot of her religion.

This was indeed the right move in the context of nineteenth-century American Protestantism. For in fact people had rejected the old laws and institutions of Puritanism, however perfect they might have been, and no arguments of Lyman Beecher or anyone else could save them. People built their lives and relationships, not on the old system of ranks and statuses—no longer mindful of their family heritage—but on contemporary associations and friendships. The enormous changes brought by the Industrial Revolution and westward migration necessitated new ways of making relationships: friendships based on common feeling, associations based on common purposes. Deep, lasting relationships could be maintained only within the family circle, the rest depended more on changing circumstance. Puritanism had depended on a stable society. Lyman helped engineer the transition, in helping to form voluntary associations to accomplish certain tasks, but those associations outstripped him, becoming a new model of religious organization entirely.

By the late nineteenth century, then, morality began not in society but at home, and even the home was experiencing great stress. Thus Harriet's appeal to the sanctity of the family aroused great depth of feeling, and her sense that slavery poisoned all American families rang true. She had transformed the deep American concern for morality—indeed, for the "government of God"—into something that late nineteenth-century Protestants could grasp. Morality meant faith, love for one's fellow beings, and a deep inner sense of right action. Uncle Tom and little Eva were those saintly creatures born with that religious and moral sense. Those who worked for the freedom of the slaves were involved in the struggle to "feel right," as Harriet put it, and then act accordingly. Likewise, the characters of *The Minister's Wooing* were engaged in a struggle to feel right, to get their religion in tune with their feeling, and then to act rightly as well.

Harriet Beecher Stowe thus helped to articulate a transformation of religion for her time. As the king of Spain and the monks of Cluny helped transform Spanish nationalism and popular fervor for pilgrimage into a new ideal that welded Christian devotion to a knightly model, so Harriet and the other popular religious writers of her time transformed Puritan moral passion and popular experiential religion into a new ideal, welding Christian beliefs to a feminine mode of feeling and sensitivity. Placed next to one another, the contrast between the two is striking: how remarkable that these could both be Christian popular movements, so different in their contexts and their formulations of the Christian ideal!

Yet a closer look reveals that the two, though certainly different, share a certain kinship. Whether consciously or not, the Cluniac monks were taming forms of energy new in their society—the power of the warrior class that, in its lust for the "joys of war," was a threat to the fragile Christian order of society; and the emergence of a kind of proto-nationalism in Spain, a pocket of independence from the Roman church that also could have threatened the fragile unity of religion in Europe. Honoring the Spanish legends of Saint James, they incorporated the Spanish spirit into the universal church, and simultaneously, they honored the knightly spirit by encouraging pilgrims to visit that Saint James who appeared in the midst of battles to help the Christian warrior. Both nationalism and the warrior spirit thereby submitted to the church and to the devotional ideals of Cluny and Rome. Indeed, the pilgrim ideal was just at that time developing into almost an order, a mildly ascetic discipline of its own.

Nineteenth-century America also faced the outpouring of enormous new energies—sometimes toward war and conquest, as in the Mexican War and the Indian wars. Contemporaries saw those energies, however, not as a dangerous military spirit but as the unruliness of freedom, throwing off old institutions that had become burdensome, expanding into new territory and experimenting with new ways of life. The dangers, as each followed his or her own opinion, came in sectarianism, factionalism, political divisions that threatened to split the new nation. The great division that epitomized them all was between North and South. Harriet Beecher Stowe and others like her provided models for healing the spirit, for finding the deeper unity underneath the factions and divisions. For her, the model was the family, held together by the love of the woman. This represented the fusion of the ideal of the perfect society, which Americans all hoped to build, with openness to individual feeling, which could occur within the loving and supportive framework of the family. Moreover, the family was one place where common feeling could be shared. Harriet's work did not avert the great division, as she had hoped; soon the nation was embroiled in civil war. Yet it did help to bring people into a sense of shared purpose and, at the same time, a sense that in grounding themselves in their deepest, purest feelings they were submitting to God. The turbulent passions of the nineteenth century found a Christian ideal, a Christian place to rest, in the symbols of home, family, and self-sacrificing love.

The two examples we have considered, so widely separated in space, time, and meaning, are similar in that they both demonstrate the Christian effort to bring human energies and drives into the framework of Christian devotion. Whether the institution that embodies that devotion be the Roman church or the American family, the pilgrimage to Saint James or the Antislavery Society, the goal is similar: to give over one's human desires to higher ideals, to sacrifice some of one's deeds in order to sanctify one's greatest values. To be sure, each culture will define differently the nature of the ideal and which desires and urges are problematic, but the model remains in many ways the same: the dynamics of Christian life involves directing one's worldly hopes, dreams, and actions to a higher purpose and thereby transforming one's life according to a higher ideal.

■

CHAPTER V

Conclusions

I n some ways, we have come full circle. In our historical treatment of Christianity, we observed how an apocalyptic Jewish sect, expecting the return of the Messiah and living a high spiritual life, evolved into the religion of a great empire. In each succeeding period, some strove to bring religious commitment and belief to a higher level, to rise to greater holiness: the monks of fourth-century Egypt, the holy men of fourth- and fifth-century Syria, the battling iconoclasts and monks of the eighth-century Eastern empire; the Benedictines of eighth-century Europe; the Cluniac monks of the tenth to twelfth centuries—on and on down to the Pentecostal churches of our own day. Whether within the established church or as critics of it, Christians have sought a life of greater holiness for themselves and, usually, for the Christian community and the society at large.

Even when we look at the enduring structures of Christianity we find the same stretching toward holiness. Baptism becomes of minor importance when it no longer marks a distinct separation between the Christian and the world. The Eucharist is hedged about with greater distance and ritual complexities, protecting its holiness. Penance becomes a central sacrament when Christians feel too contaminated by the world; gaining forgiveness of sins becomes a constant preoccupation. To the Reformers of the sixteenth century, the entire system seems corrupt; there is too much emphasis on "works," on what the individual can do for him- or herself. They urge a return to the original purity, the holiness, of the Book, and to the inward relationship of the individual with God. The inward quest becomes the new direction of purity and holiness in modern times.

We saw in detail how this dynamic operated in the two examples we examined in Chapter IV, how each new burst of human energies was tamed and channeled, through a reimagining of Christian ideals, into a path of spiritual excellence. Even in times when the unity of Christianity seems to have disintegrated, when the supposedly enduring structures no longer endure, the attempt to transform life in the direction of greater spirituality, greater perfection, continues. One of the central assertions of early Christianity was that, because Jesus died for the sins of humanity, salvation was possible. We understood that to mean that transformation was possible: one could live a higher life, a more nearly perfect life, approaching the divine.

Yet in emphasizing this transformative energy of Christianity, this direction to holiness, we night be in danger of losing some of the distinctiveness of Christianity. Many religions have this dynamic—perhaps all of them, to one degree or another. The quest for holiness, the yearning for perfection, the desire simply to live a "good life" in the midst of evil, are all aspects of a basic religious impulse. Christianity has the same motivation, but with its own peculiar character. The churches have asserted that what is involved in the transformation toward perfection is not only a change in one's behavior but a change in the quality of one's whole state of being. Particularly, it involves a divorce from the material side of one's nature and a turn to the spiritual. This appears most strongly in the ascetic strands of Christianity, but it is present throughout; unlike adherents of many religious traditions, Christians often enter into battle with the material, with the "flesh" that hinders the spirit. Moreover, such a divorce and such a transformation are possible, Christians have claimed, only because of the saving act of God in Jesus Christ. Left to themselves, people remain enmeshed in sin and temptation, deeply wounded in spirit by sin. In a great mystery, God acting in Jesus removed the effects of sin for those who believe, making possible a true and complete transformation—so that, as it were, not the least scar remains.

The quest for holiness in Christianity, therefore, has been intertwined with a belief in the miracle and the necessity of Christ having come to earth, died, and been resurrected. The mystery is never resolved by rational attempts to understand it; it is simply believed. And the mystery becomes a model: self-sacrifice, following in Jesus' steps, becomes prominent in many strands of the tradition. The idea and practice of sacrifice is significant in many religions, and in

Christianity it is of course derived in part from the idea and practice of sacrifice in Judaism. But the image of personal sacrifice has dominated more than it has in other religions. The martyrs of the early centuries, the monks from Anthony to Francis, the pietists fascinated with the blood of Jesus, Harriet Beecher Stowe with her self-sacrificing, all-loving and forgiving characters—all these are dramatically Christian, with the figure of the crucified Jesus hovering in the background. Holiness in Christianity is most frequently intertwined with the idea of personal sacrifice—of property, of desires, of one's very life.

Yet Christianity has undergone enormous change over the centuries. One might question, for example, whether self-sacrifice is an important as it was a century, or five centuries, ago. Even more, one can ask whether people calling themselves Christians believe in the great mystery of the saving death of Christ, or do they instead see Jesus mainly as a great teacher? And if there is a quest for holiness, is there really one distinctively Christian way? It would seem that there are too many churches offering too many different versions of the Christian life. The problems facing modern Christianity thus require some discussion, at least to put the issues as clearly as possible. For in fact these issues are not entirely or necessarily unique to Christianity in modern times; we can find similar issues throughout Christian history.

Probably the most pervasive issue facing modern Christians is the fact of religious pluralism, within and outside the boundaries of Christianity itself. This is not new—diversity within Christianity is as old as the religion itself, and Christianity grew up in an environment of many religions. What is new—essentially since the late eighteenth century—is the acceptance and tolerance of diversity within the ranks. Whereas Christians in earlier times fought desperately to assert the superiority of their version of the faith, to prove that theirs was the one true way, modern Christians have accepted the existence of a variety of Christianities. The outward framework for this has been the **ecumenical** movement, the association of churches to share ideas and cooperate on work where they can agree. Shortly after the turn of the century, a number of American denominations formed the Federal Council of Churches; later they re-formed as the National Council of Churches and gradually joined with churches in other lands to form the World Council of

Churches. Not all denominations belong; indeed, some conservative groups who thought the council was too liberal have formed alternative organizations. Still, however, the ecumenical spirit is present, and the joint work has enabled the churches to accomplish social work and missionary efforts that would have been beyond the capacity of individual churches.

Nevertheless, the ecumenical movement skirts the issue that lies at the root of the problem of pluralism: the issue of truth. Is there one theology or way of thinking about Christianity? Is there one path to God that is better than the others? Are there a few basics, at least, that we can say Christians must agree on in order to consider themselves truly Christian? Particularly in a religion that traditionally has emphasized doctrine or belief, this would seem an important issue. Yet at present, neither theological faculties in seminaries nor bishops in council nor lay believers, with their involvement in daily practice, are moving toward any new agreement. Except in Fundamentalist churches, there has been a move away from relying on doctrine, so new developments may not come through great theological syntheses. Additionally, Christians have renewed their interest in ritual, especially since Vatican II; possibly the ancient sacraments may provide a new basis for unity. But nothing is certain; it is not even clear that most Christians feel any strong need for greater unification in the faith.

The issue is accentuated by the greater presence today of non-Christian religions in Europe and the United States. This larger pluralism has led Christians to learn more about other religions of the world. When in 1893 the World Parliament of Religions met in Chicago, most Christian leaders came away assured that Christianity was undoubtedly the most advanced religion in the world. Now, faced with a population intensely interested in other religions, encountering radically different assumptions about the nature of the universe, human nature, the goals of human life, and the means to achieve these goals, Christian scholars and teachers have had to take a different posture. It is not so easy to say, as Origen did in the third century, that Christianity represents the climax of civilization. Today the question must be asked whether Christianity—any of the Christianities—offers a way of holiness distinctive enough from other religions to make special claims on believers. Moreover, the modern attitude of tolerance makes it rather impolite to claim such specialness. Whereas Jews, Christians, and Muslims in the Middle Ages argued with intent to win, today Christians (and representatives of other religions) may prefer to take the attitude that people choose a religion according to their individual tastes. This does not accommodate well to the traditional belief that Christ came to save all humanity, that Christian claims are true universally, for everyone at all times. Yet it may be one of the advances—or casualties, depending on one's perspective—of modern times to see Christianity as one among many religious options.

Another problem, related to but separable from the problems of pluralism, is that of disbelief. As we observed earlier, Christianity has to a remarkable degree depended on belief as an integral part of faith—belief in a specific creed or doctrine, engaging the intellect in the act of faith. The past few centuries have brought developments in philosophy and the sciences that have called into question some of the fundamental doctrines that most Christians have held through the ages. Evolutionary theory in geology and biology have questioned the literal truth of the Bible, especially the story of creation, and archaeology and historical studies have strongly suggested that many of the accounts in the Bible are legendary, or at least that "history" has been greatly modified by the authors' points of view. Some of the sayings of Jesus appear not to be sayings of Jesus at all, but traditions of the church. The general scientific world view, with its belief in laws of nature, has led many Christians to question the miracles of Jesus and special divine interventions like the virgin birth or the immaculate conception of Mary.

Again, intellectual challenges to the faith are not new. The introduction of Aristotle into the schools in the twelfth and thirteenth centuries created a furor not unlike the modern arguments over scientific theory. Greek ideas seemed to threaten the very foundation of Christian faith. The issues were resolved only by Aquinas's new, and for that time daring, synthesis, which preserved the doctrines while incorporating the philosophical strengths of Aristotle's position. Today it is a question whether a new philosophical strategy could also preserve the doctrines in their classic form. Doctrines themselves may have to be reinterpreted, using what scholars have learned about the deeper meanings of myth and legend, for example, or what psychological theories have to say about the work of religious symbols and rites in human consciousness. The advantage of the challenges is the same as in the twelfth century: a major work of education will likely be stimulated, both in the seminaries and among the lay believers in the churches.

There are many other issues we could consider, but we will content ourselves with just one more: the problem of experiential Christianity. We have observed that since the Reformation, and especially in the past two hundred years, Christians have focused increasingly on the individual's personal experience as the center, and sometimes the measure, of Christianity. This contributed to the breakdown of traditional communities and the corporate conception of the church and led to voluntarism, which in turn contributed to the growth of sectarian, pluralistic Christianity. These represent dangers to a traditional model of the Christian church. However, there is a problem with experiential Christianity itself. Experience, by its nature (excluding telepathic perception), cannot be shared directly; it must be communicated in language, gesture, or art. Deep feelings, profound religious experiences, are, as the great mystics have observed, very difficult to communicate. The religious experience and the stages of it tend to take forms, to become formalized, in a way that is diametrically opposed to the ideal of experiential religion—namely, that each person find his or her own way to God. Thus the stages of mysticism were formalized, the process of Puritan conversion became a rigid standard, the testimonials of nineteenth-century revivals became clichés. Some modern Christians, in reaction to such developments, have turned to ethics as the core of the religion. Others have simply ignored the problem, trusting that each individual will be sincere about his or her own faith.

Yet it is not a question of sincerity, but one of spiritual growth. One can be sincere about one's feelings and still not know what to do with them, or how to act on them, except to follow the prescriptions of one's group. This can result—in some cases has resulted—in a highly conformist religious practice and belief, even while the group continues to preach individuality. This, of course, is a problem in any religion that takes as its foundation the individual's experience rather than some common ritual or commonly experienced event. Other religions, for example Buddhism, have dealt with the problem by introducing another factor: the spiritual teacher. The teacher, involved intimately with the student yet far more experienced in exploring the inner life, can be a guide in development. In

Christianity, the abbot often served this purpose for the monks; the mystics had their circles in which one person usually served as guide for the others; in Puritanism the pastor was supposed to play this role. (In secular life today the psychotherapist guides the person in inner development, though it does not always include spiritual development.) In most modern forms of Christianity, however, the individual is bereft of experienced spiritual leadership. Conformity, shallowness, and ultimately dissatisfaction is often the outcome. Modern Christianity sometimes covers this dissatisfaction with involvement in external affairs—missions, charitable work, social occasions for gathering together. It remains to be seen whether it will become a serious problem in the years ahead.

Christianity is not alone in facing these problems, of course. All religions face pluralism on a large scale; all must deal with hard questions of disbelief in a society immersed in rational philosophy, scientific culture, and critical historical studies. All, too, must face the issues of experiential versus externally grounded religion; each type has its own difficulties. Christians must face such issues in their own distinctive way, reflecting on their traditions, returning to their resources in the Bible, religious thought, and practice, while at the same time developing as deep an understanding of each issue as possible. In that continuing dialogue of the Christian religion with its culture, in the ongoing struggle to define Christian existence, the Christian quest for perfection will continue.

Notes

1. Our calendar is based on the Christian custom, introduced in the sixth century and formalized by Pope Hadrian I about 780 C.E., of dating from the birth of Jesus (the "year of our Lord," *anno Domini* in Latin, or A.D.). Scholars have recently introduced the abbreviation C.E. for "of the common era" or "Christian era," since other religions have their own calendars. B.C.E., or "before the common era," replaces B.C.

2. Paul's authentic letters are Romans, First and Second Corinthians, Galatians, Ephesians, Colossians, First (and possibly Second) Thessalonians, and Philippians. The Gospels were most probably written in the following order: Mark (ca. 65–70 C.E.), Matthew (ca 85), Luke/Acts (ca. 90–95), John (ca. 90–100); the exact dates are disputed.

3. It seems likely that Cluny's emphasis on the *opus Dei* (the "work of God," i.e., the liturgy of the divine office) may have been encouraged by the influence of monks from the Eastern church. In the ninth, tenth, and eleventh centuries some Byzantine monks fled the Arab invasions of Sicily and Italy and went north, taking refuge in Western monasteries. The mystical emphasis of the East may thus have contributed to Cluny's focus on the proper worship of God: Cluniac monks were expected to spend as much waking time in collective prayer as in all their other activities combined.

4. Some Christian traditions have claimed that this meal was actually the Passover seder, celebrated on the first night of the holiday. This is highly unlikely, as the courts would not have been in session to try Jesus on the following day; moreover, nothing in the nature of the meal mentioned suggests the elaborate Passover celebration. It is possible that Jesus was tried only by a Roman court, not a Jewish one, but that calls into question other parts of the New Testament accounts.

5. Originally the Eucharist was a regular meal, but its center was the repetition of the crucial acts of Jesus at the Last Supper. There, tradition records, Jesus blessed and broke bread according to Jewish custom while saying to his disciples, "Take; this is my body." On blessing the wine cup at the end of the meal he said, "This is my blood of the covenant, which is poured out for many" (Mark 14:22–24). The church understood that this was to be repeated, as a powerful remembrance of Jesus: it re-called, invoked the very presence of Jesus in the bread and wine. This central part became the core of the Eucharist.

The rest of the meal was separated off, becoming the *agape* or love-feast, a communal meal; eventually that part was dropped, leaving the drama of the Eucharist itself.

6. Georges Duby, *The Making of the Christian West, 980–1100* (New York: World Publishing Co., 1967), p. 25.

7. Ignatius, *Letter to the Romans*, 2.2, 4.1,2.

8. Pelayo was also the name of a nationalist Spanish hero in a battle against the Muslims in 718; this man was reputed also to live in caves and eat only honey, like the later Pelayo.

9. Quoted from *Codex Calixtinus*, bk. 5, in Horton and Marie-Helène Davies, *Holy Days and Holidays: The Medieval Pilgrimage to Compostela* (Lewisburg, Pa.: Bucknell University Press, 1982), pp. 213, 215.

10. Lyman Beecher, "A Reformation of Morals Practicable and Indispensable," in *Lyman Beecher and the Reform of Society* (New York: Arno Press, 1972), p. 22.

11. *Ibid.*, p. 15.

12. Harriet Beecher Stowe, *The Minister's Wooing* (Ridgewood, N.J.: Gregg Press, 1968; originally published, 1859), pp. 23, 54.

Glossary

Apocalypse. A Jewish or Christian writing from the period 200 B.C.E. to 150 C.E. prophesying in vivid symbolism the imminent end of the world.

Apology. A formal defense of the Christian faith.

Apostle. One of the earliest missionaries commissioned to preach the gospel; traditionally, twelve are counted (Jesus' twelve disciples), plus Paul, the "apostle to the Gentiles (non-Jews)."

Baptism. The rite of ritual immersion which initiated a person into the Christian church. At first, full immersion was used as in Jewish conversions; later, pouring or sprinkling with water came into use in some churches.

Bishop. The rank in Roman Catholic and Eastern Orthodox churches above a priest, with authority to ordain priests as well as perform other sacraments. In the early church, an elected head of the church for an entire city; now, an appointed head of a diocese. (A few other churches, such as the Methodist and Mormon, also have the office of bishop.)

Born again. In modern Christianity, having experienced a true conversion and/or total dedication to Christ, usually in an intense emotional experience.

Cardinal. An official in the Roman Catholic church next below the pope, appointed by the pope as a member of the "college" of cardinals which was formed in the Middle Ages to assist the pope and elect new popes.

Catechism. Originally, oral instruction in doctrine; can mean any official summary of doctrine used to teach newcomers to the faith.

Catechumen. One receiving instruction in basic doctrines before baptism or, if already baptized as an infant, before confirmation or first Communion.

Circumcision. A rite in which a piece of skin near the tip of a male's penis is removed with a knife; in Judaism, the sign of the covenant between God on the one hand, and Abraham and his descendants on the other.

Clergy. The body of ordained men (and in some churches women) in a church, permitted to perform the priestly and/or pastoral duties.

Communion. The Christian sacrament of receiving bread and wine as the body and blood of Christ (or as symbols thereof).

Confirmation. A rite admitting a baptized person into full church membership, originally by anointing with oil.

Conviction. In modern Christianity, the state in which one recognizes one's sinfulness and guilt before God, preliminary to experiencing conversion.

Deacon. The lowest ordained office in the Roman Catholic church (together with subdeacon), originally in charge of gathering and distributing the Eucharistic offerings, later a stage in seminary training. In modern Protestant churches, a deacon may be an official elected to a certain responsibility in worship or administration.

Dogma. A church's authoritative statement of belief; doctrine.

Ecumenical. Promoting a worldwide Christian unity or cooperation.

Elect. Those chosen by God for eternal life, according to theological systems which believe in predestination.

Elevation of the host. The priestly practice of raising the Eucharistic bread above the head so that the laypeople behind the priest can see it, at the moment of transubstantiation.

Eschatology. A theory of the end of the world, how and when it will occur, and what the end times will be like.

Eucharist. The Christian sacrament of receiving bread and wine as the body and blood of Christ. This term is more often used for the sacrament in the Catholic and Orthodox churches, "Communion" in the Protestant.

Evangelical, evangelizing. Those churches or movements that emphasize preaching to repentance and conversion; in modern Christianity, their beliefs usually include salvation by faith and emphasis on scripture as well as a conversion experience.

Excommunication. The act of church authorities to deprive a person of church membership, specifically the right to take Communion.

Friars. From the Latin word for brothers, members of one of the mendicant (begging) orders as distinct from the cloistered monks.

Grace. Unmerited divine assistance on one's spiritual path; often conceived as a special blessing received in an intense experience, but also may include a sense of special direction in one's life.

Holy Spirit. In Judaism, the presence of God as evidenced in the speech of the prophets and other divine manifestations; in Christianity, understood more generally as the active, guiding presence of God in the church and its members.

Icon. A painted religious image—for example of Mary, Christ, or a saint—understood in Eastern Orthodoxy to be a copy of a heavenly image.

Immaculate Conception. Conceiving a baby, namely the Virgin Mary, under a special dispensation so that she remained pure, without the original sin usually transmitted through the sexual act. Feasts celebrating her conception were popular in the Middle Ages, although the official doctrine was not declared by the pope until 1854.

Inquisition. Roman Catholic tribunal for investigating and punishing heresy. The first papal Inquisitions began in the late twelfth century and were centralized under Innocent III; another famous tribunal was the Spanish Inquisition in the fifteenth and sixteenth centuries.

Justification. The state of being released by God from the guilt of sin.

Kingdom of God. The state of the world in which God's will is fulfilled; expected to be brought into being at the end of time when Christ returns.

Liturgy. Rites of public worship, usually institutionalized in church tradition.

Mass. The entire set of prayers and ceremonies surrounding the Eucharist.

Messiah. Literally, the "anointed one" of God (*Christos* in Greek, Christ in English); God's chosen king, expected to bring peace, prosperity, and perfection to the world.

Millenarian. Having to do with the expected millennium, or thousand-year reign of Christ prophesied in Revelation, a time in which the world would be brought to perfection. Millenarian movements often grow up around predictions that this perfect time is about to begin.

Monasticism. The way of life or tradition of monks or nuns living in monasteries, that is, houses established to support a celibate, disciplined, and intensely religious way of life.

Mystical, mysticism. Aspects of religion which emphasize the individual's quest for union or direct communion with God.

Ordination. Ceremony of investing a person with ministerial or priestly office.

Original sin. The fundamental state of sin, inherited from the first man Adam, which according to most Christian theology infects all of humanity if not saved by Christ.

Patriarch. One of the bishops of the four major early Christian centers—Rome, Jerusalem, Antioch, or Alexandria, with Constantinople later added as a fifth. After the break with Rome, the term may refer to the head of any of the national divisions of the Eastern church.

Penance. The sacramental rite, in Roman Catholicism, consisting of repentance, confession to a priest, payment of the temporal penalty for one's sins, and forgiveness.

Predestination. The idea that one's eternal destiny is determined beforehand, from the beginning of time, by God's will.

Purgatory. An intermediate state after death, according to Roman Catholic theology, where one can finish satisfying the temporal punishments for one's sins and purify one's soul before being admitted to heaven.

Relics. Objects or parts of the body (e.g., clothing, teeth, bones) left behind after the decay of the corpse, which are venerated for saints of the Roman Catholic and Eastern churches.

Resurrection. Rising from the dead, with a restored bodily form.

Revivals. Events of spiritual awakening or high religious interest; specifically in modern Christianity, special meetings to encourage such awakening or interest.

Sacrament. A formal religious rite regarded as sacred for its perfect ability to convey divine blessing; in some traditions (especially Protestant), it is regarded as not effective in itself but as a sign or symbol of spiritual reality.

Salvation. Most generally, liberation from the power and effects of sin; often refers to an experience or series of experiences leading to a sense of liberation; sometimes refers to the expected liberation of a Christian after death.

Sin. A transgression or offense against God's laws or wishes; more generally in Christian belief, a continuing state of estrangement from God.

Tongues. An ecstatic utterance while in a state of religious excitation; sometimes regarded as a special spiritual language or ability to speak in different languages.

Transubstantiation. The change, during the Eucharist, of the substance of bread and wine into the substance of Christ's body and blood. According to Roman Catholic theology, the "accidents" (taste, color, shape) of the elements remain the same, but the substance changes into the holy elements of the sacrifice.

Trinity. God the Father, Christ the Son, and the Holy Spirit in perfect unity, as three "persons" in one God. The nature of this union was much debated in the early church, and Western and Eastern understandings differ.

Virgin. Mary, the mother of Jesus, held since early times to have conceived and given birth to Jesus without losing her virginity.

Selected Reading List

This list includes a sampling of surveys as well as interesting studies of specific topics, but is by no means fully representative. Most of the studies below include bibliographies to direct the student to other resources.

Ahlstrom, Sydney. *A Religious History of the American People*. New Haven: Yale University Press, 1972.

Albanese, Catherine. *America: Religion and Religions*. Wadsworth Publishing, 1981.

Benz, Ernst. *The Eastern Orthodox Church*. New York: Doubleday, 1957.

Brown, Peter. *The Cult of Saints*. Chicago: University of Chicago Press, 1982.

———. *The Making of Late Antiquity*. Cambridge: Harvard University Press, 1978.

Dix, Dom Gregory. *The Shape of the Liturgy*. New York: Winston Press (reprint), 1982.

Duby, Georges. *The Making of the Christian West 980–1140*. New York: World Publishing, 1967.

Foster, Lawrence. *Religion and Sexuality: Three Communal Experiments of the Nineteenth Century*. Chicago: University of Chicago Press, 1980.

Gager, John. *Kingdom and Community: A Social History of Early Christianity*. Englewood Cliffs, N.J.: Prentice-Hall, 1975.

———. *The Origins of Anti-Semitism*. New York: Oxford University Press, 1983.

Knowles, David. *The Evolution of Medieval Thought*. New York: Random House, 1964.

Lossky, Vladimir. *The Meaning of Icons*. Boston: Palmer, 1956.

Male, Emile. *Religious Art from the Twelfth to the Eighteenth Century*. Princeton, N.J.: Princeton University Press, 1982.

Marty, Martin. *Christianity in the New World*. N.Y.: Winston Press, 1984.

McKenzie, John L. *The Roman Catholic Church*. New York: Doubleday, 1969.

Ozment, Steven E. *The Age of Reform*. New Haven: Yale University Press, 1980.

Placher, William C. *A History of Christian Theology: An Introduction*. Philadelphia: Westminster Press, 1983.

Raboteau, Albert J. *Slave Religion: The Invisible Institution in the Antebellum South*. New York: Oxford University Press, 1980.

Sizer, Sandra S. *Gospel Hymns and Social Religion: The Rhetoric of Nineteenth Century Revivalism*. Philadelphia: Temple University Press, 1978.

Southern, Richard W. *The Making of the Middle Ages*. New Haven: Yale University Press, 1953.

Ullmann, Walter. *A Short History of the Papacy in the Middle Ages*. New York: Methven, Inc., 1974.

Williams, Georges Huntston. *The Radical Reformation*. Philadelphia: Westminster Press, 1962.

Zernov, Nicholas. *Eastern Christendom*. London: Reader's Union, 1963.